Sisters in Arms

Sisters in Arms

This book is dedicated to all Ack Ack girl Gunners who served in World War Two.

The author wishes to acknowledge her debt to the author of the following work of reference:

General Sir Frederick Pile GCB DSO MC GOC in Command

ACK ACK

Britain's Defence Against Air Attack during the Second World War.

HarperCollins Publishers
77-85 Fulham Palace Road
Hammersmith
London W6 8JB

Published by HarperCollins Publishers, 1996
Reprint 1 3 5 7 9   8 6 4 2

ISBN 0 00 472084 9

Printed and bound in Great Britain by Caledonian International Book Manufacturing Ltd, Glasgow, G64.

Contents

Foreword

Choosing recipients for a Noel's Christmas Present from the thousands of nominations is always a difficult task. However, when we heard about the extraordinary achievements of Vee Robinson, we knew we had found an unsung heroine, a human dynamo with amazing talents. She has ensured that many of the women who served in the last war in the anti-aircraft batteries remain in contact and get together for reunions. Vee has also written this account of her wartime experiences. It has been her dream to have this book published to a wide audience.

I am delighted to turn Vee's dream into reality. Thanks are due to everyone associated with the publishing, printing and distribution of *Sisters in Arms*. Thanks also to you for buying a copy. Every copy sold includes a donation to the Royal Artillery Heritage fund, a cause very close to Vee's heart. And finally, many thanks must go to Vee for writing this book and being the inspiration for this very special Christmas Present.

Noel Edmonds
BBC Television
December 1996

Introduction

As a regular soldier with seven years' service in when World War Two started, to put it mildly I was a trifle concerned when in 1941 it was decided to form mixed-sex Heavy Anti-Aircraft batteries.

Girls from all walks of life volunteered to train as gunners and relieve men for overseas duty. Thousands of them responded magnificently to the call. They learned quickly and were always cheerful: there were times when being cheerful was extremely difficult. The girls were proud of what they were doing and of being granted the privilege of wearing the R A Grenade along with the white lanyard plus the Artillery flash on their "tin hats".

They proved their worth and served with the guns alongside men. They had arrived as gunners.

R G Wilson, Ex. Sergeant. R A –

On Looking Back

The noise was deafening. Great heavy anti-aircraft guns were blasting away non-stop and the acrid smell of cordite was all around. Strange looking objects filled the sky with tails of flame, sounding like ancient motorcycles. Royal Air Force fighter planes were over the sea chasing the fiendish robot-type things and the noise of their machine guns added to the sickening din: it was an inferno.

The sounds grew fainter, I opened my eyes to find my fingers tightly gripping the top bar of a metal field gate, my knuckles were white. Slowly, I uncurled my fingers and looked across Romney Marsh. Sheep and lambs made white blobs on the rolling green pasture; the sky was blue with fluffy clouds. A lark sang as it rose from almost beneath my feet. I watched till it was out of sight. The far-off hum of a tractor could be heard and a soft wind sighing – peaceful sounds. It was vivid memory that evoked a moment ago sights and sounds of the time when I was here before on this marshland. For then it bristled with guns, a formidable barrage along the south coast of England, and khaki-clad figures wore steel helmets day and night.

The scene before me now was idyllic and could well have been a backdrop in an old-fashioned film where any minute the hero or heroine would come into view. It couldn't have been more of a contrast from the first scene. Heroes and heroines did walk here, though all of them are unsung.

By the time I was in action on Romney Marsh, however, I had been part of a mixed Heavy Anti-Aircraft Battery for three years. The Battery had defended areas in the northeast of

England and in Scotland against enemy planes – Hitler's famous Luftwaffe, intent on dropping their lethal loads on Air, Naval and Army installations and the inhabitants of cities. The German Intelligence appeared to be well informed.

Mixed batteries were formed from scratch consisting of girls from the age of eighteen upwards, who had done only four weeks basic training. Volunteers from all kinds of backgrounds, who had been taught to march, wear uniform correctly and salute the King's commissioned officers smartly, had been inspected, injected, tested and physically graded. They were then given a rail warrant to wherever their next phase of training happened to be.

Royal Artillery training barracks housed girls for the first time – apart from the NAAFI (Navy, Army and Air Force Institute) girls who worked in the canteen, that is. They had, however, less spartan quarters than the ATS (Auxiliary Territorial Service) girls who were soon to be soldiers. The ATS girls were trained alongside the men, the batteries being formed at the beginning of the training.

The men, for the most part, except for officers and senior NCOs who were regular soldiers, were much older than the girls and had been members of the peacetime Territorial Army. There were also a few regular gunners who had been physically downgraded after being wounded in the fighting overseas, and after hospital treatment were posted to form mixed batteries. Without exception, not one of the soldiers relished the thought of working with girls, least of all the officers who would be responsible for the smooth running of the operation. This, after all, was totally without precedent and only resorted to because of the situation regarding the shortage of manpower overseas. The maxim "desperate situations call for desperate measures" was never truer.

I was on a sentimental journey (though perhaps sentimental wasn't the right word), reviving memories good and bad by visiting all the gunsites on which I had served in World War Two – that slice out of my life spent away from home wearing khaki battledress. Leaning over the gate that April day, enjoying the utter peace and tranquillity, I wept. I couldn't have explained why. Tears trickled down my face. My emotions were mixed:

sadness for things long gone, regret, thankfulness and pride. Pride – yes, for with thousands of other girls I had helped defend this land of ours against an enemy who threatened us with slavery. That may sound melodramatic; nevertheless it was true. War is not glorious, whatever has been written about it. War is horrendous and has no place in a civilised world.

My mind went back to the events which had led up to my being here in that line of defence so long ago.

I lived in Arley, a Warwickshire village; the nearest town was Nuneaton; the city of Coventry lay a few miles further to the south. At school, many had fathers who had fought in the "war to end all wars" which ended in 1918: stories were still being written about the battles fought in the Great War. On Armistice Day, which was always a special day at school, we'd boast about our dads. The regiments they had been in, the wounds they had received; if we were all to be believed then our village held more heroes than any other. Some of the boasting was justified, for more than one still suffered from the effects of mustard gas and two of the fathers walked with a limp. Great was the kudos of a child whose father was such a victim. To us it was all so long ago and we, so young, were ignorant of the real savagery of war.

The threat of another outbreak of war was looming. Germany had been breaking agreements regarding rearmament and crossing borders unhindered since 1936. By 1937 the British Army High Command were sure that war was on its way; there was talk of rearming but not much was done. The fist Anti-Aircraft Division consisted mainly of part-time soldiers – the Territorial Army. The controlling instrument for guns was the same vintage as that used in 1918 and the total number of anti-aircraft guns in Britain was one hundred and forty-six. By 1939 more were being manufactured and it was then that Anti-Aircraft Command came into being with General Frederick Pile (later to become Sir Frederick) at its head. An army scientific establishment was formed then to assist and advise on the many technical problems to be faced. General Pile was determined that Ack Ack Command would eventually become the most highly technical unit that ever wore khaki.

It wasn't until Hitler set his sights on Poland that the British government shook itself from its torpor and rumbled to its feet to protest; in vain. Air Raid Precautions (ARP) came into being; preparations were begun to evacuate children and mothers with babies from the cities.

The possibility of war was on everyone's lips. Fathers discussed it in pubs and at work, some said it would never happen, some thought it would, others said that no one would dare to go to war with Great Britain and the rest said that Britain ought to do something to stop the Germans from taking over all Europe, for it looked as if that is what they intended to do. Mothers talked worriedly in shops and on buses.

"Oh no, it won't happen, my husband says it won't."

"No, of course it won't," agreed others, lulling themselves into believing it wouldn't because they said so. The realists who had read newspaper reports with more intellect admitted to themselves that they were fearful.

In August 1939 Britain sent a message to Hitler, saying that Britain would stand by Poland whatever the consequences. Gas masks were issued, ARP members had to cajole some passive citizens into collecting theirs from distribution points, for many people still thought even then that war could be averted. By August 31st no answers from Hitler had been received. The Royal Navy was mobilised, Army and Royal Air Force reserves called up.

On the first day of September the evacuation of children began and the first heartbreaking separations keenly felt. Britain's children, poor little mites from the larger cities, many of them too young to understand, were gathered on railway platforms in hundreds, all wearing labels round their necks. Even the older ones could hardly be expected to know why they were being taken away from their parents. The operation was fraught with difficulties; never had such an undertaking been attempted before. Some children ran away from their new homes and tried to find their way back to the ones they had tearfully left. In some cases the mothers kept the children with them, others took them back to safety: it was an unhappy time.

Hitler's army invaded the Polish border, Warsaw (the capital) was bombed. Even after that, there were still people in Britain with their heads in the sand saying that it wouldn't happen, but it could and it did.

On Sunday September 3rd at 11 a.m. Neville Chamberlain, the Prime Minister, broadcast to the nation. In homes all over the land, from cottages to stately homes, that sunny Sunday morning we listened in silence to his words of doom. Every single one of us knew from that moment that our lives would be changed. We were at war with Germany, again.

The last war had never been forgotten, some indeed were still suffering from its effects and many of those who had fought in it would have to fight again: sons too – many of them were of an age to be called upon to serve their country. Bitterly they talked, those who had survived to build a home and rear children through all the hard time of the post-war years, and for what! To provide cannon fodder for German guns once again.

One old man in our village on the evening of that historic day was heard to say, after listening to all the arguments and predictions of the know-alls, "Well we're at war so we'll just ha' to gerron wi' it same as last time."

"It's all right for you old 'un," one of the younger men said, "you ain't gonna be the one that'll ha' to go out and face them bloody Jerries."

"Yer young bugger," the old man retorted, "who'll stop 'em if we don't? Gie up talking like an old washerwoman and gerroff yer backside, don't wait till they ha' to come for yer. Volunteer tomorrer, I would if I thought they'd 'av me."

The saying "Well we're at war so we'll just ha' to gerron wi' it" became a catch phrase from then on. It was quoted when anyone was heard to grumble, which was often during the days that followed. Someone had only to start, "Well we're at war ... " for everyone nearby to chorus, "so we'll just ha' to gerron wi' it." Even the grumbler sometimes finished the phrase. The old man in the pub that night of the 3rd of September little knew that his philosophy would bring a few smiles and laughter in the days ahead, and "Gerron wi' it" everyone had to.

Food and petrol were rationed. Lord Woolton was the Minister of Food; he was responsible for some of the menus in the Ministry of Food leaflets which were issued from time to time. At first only five items of food were rationed – bacon, ham, butter, sugar and meat. Later on, as merchant ships were being sunk relentlessly by the enemy, all food was rationed except offal and fish. These were in such short supply that there was never enough to go round, so whenever they were available, long queues were formed outside any shop rumoured to have any. Sometimes it was only a rumour and the housewives queued in vain. Clothes too were rationed; coupons were allocated, clothing underwent a change which had nothing to do with fashion, men's trouser turn-ups were abolished and pockets on garments were limited. Even furniture was rationed, by docket. Woolton Pie was long remembered as being one of the first recipes from the Ministry of Food leaflets and was received with mixed reactions at many a table. The dish was filling – that's all that could be said about it, apart from the expletives expressed in some households when the pie was opened!

The recipe:
1 1/2 lb. cooked mixed vegetables
2 tablespoonfuls chopped parsley
1/2 pt. stock of water
Pastry
2 oz. oatmeal
2 oz. mashed potato
2 oz. cheese
4 oz. flour
water to mix
Salt

Place cooked vegetables in pie dish and sprinkle with coarsely chopped parsley.
Add vegetable water and seasoning.
To make the pastry, cream potato with 1 oz fat, mixed grated cheese, oatmeal, flour and salt, stir into the creamed fat and potato, mix to stiff dough with water. Roll out pastry, cover pie and bake in moderate oven for 30 minutes.
Serve with jacket potatoes and green vegetables.

The egg ration was (per person) one a fortnight, with 2 oz of tea a week, 1 oz of cheese a week and milk was also rationed. Tinned goods, when available, were allocated on a points system – these could be saved and used over a period. The British housewives were faced with the difficult task of feeding their families among all the other hardships they were enduring.

Carrot marmalade was another wartime recipe, I don't remember if it originated from the Food Office or whether it was published in one of the magazines or newspapers which printed helpful hints and advice on food. All kinds of concoctions were experimented with and passed on to their readers. Instructions also were given for making clothes out of anything which a sewing needle could pierce: ingenuity was the thing. Recycling is not new and necessity is truly the mother of invention.

My friend Amy had a group of us in stitches (no pun intended) one day when she related the episode of the carrot marmalade. Her mother followed the recipe carefully for that delectable delight and with much pride placed it on the breakfast table one Sunday morning. Amy's dad who hadn't readily taken to the idea of food rationing pointed to the marmalade and said, "What's this then?"

"Marmalade," said his wife as he peered at it.

"What's in it then?" he asked.

"Well, er, it's very nutritious the recipe says."

"Yes but what's in it?" he demanded.

Amy's mother looked at her husband and said with great deliberation, "Carrots."

All of us listening were agog by this time, for we knew of his reputation; he had been known to throw his dinner on the fire, plate and all, if he wasn't suited – that even before rationing had come upon us. "Well," said Amy, "There we were sitting with bated breath expecting the fist to come crashing down on the table to rattle everything on it, his normal reaction to anything that didn't please him. Instead he got up from his chair and without saying another word picked up the jar, walked out through the kitchen door and down the garden path: you should have seen Mum's face." At this Amy burst into laughter, she was laughing so much we joined in even if we didn't think it was funny, her laughter was infectious. When we had all wiped our eyes she told us the rest. Her dad had gone to the bottom of the garden, taken off the lid from the offending jar, tipped its contents on the compost heap, hit the bottom of the jar with his hand to make sure it was empty, walked back up the path and put it carefully in the dustbin. While he was doing all this, Amy, her sister and two brothers watched from the window, darting back to their places at the table before he entered the house: no one had uttered a word. Amy continued, "Dad sat down and carried on with his meal as if nothing had happened. We weren't sure if the incident was over, so we finished our breakfast and got outside as quickly as we dared, then we hooted with laughter until the tears ran down our cheeks." Later that day their mum also enjoyed a good laugh with the four of them while her husband was safely out of the way. Even after that when she was down in the dumps, one of them only had to say, "Marmalade, Mum," and she could smile.

Arley was in a mining area and most of the men were miners. Coal mining was a reserved occupation so men in the mines were exempt from call-up into the Armed Forces. There wasn't a large exodus from our village but there were still enough young men who hadn't followed their fathers into the pit to make gaps in the community. Men were called up into one of the services between the ages of eighteen and fifty-one.

On the sixteenth day after war was declared, German raiders flew in to attack ships lying at anchor in the Firth of Forth and the Forth Bridge. An Ack Ack battery stationed at the south end of the bridge was practising gun drill when suddenly, without warning, spotters saw a German plane approaching the bridge. The gun detachment prepared to fire but the aircraft was too low. Another plane came down out of the clouds: they hit its tail fin and it crashed into the water. More planes came down through the clouds from all directions; other gunsites were then in action and three enemy raiders were shot down jointly by Ack Ack and Spitfires. No bombs fell on the dockyards but some ships were damaged and there were casualties on board.

The people of Britain prepared for more air raids; it was a war of nerves just waiting for things to happen. I can remember standing gazing up at the starlit sky on clear nights watching for enemy planes till my neck ached. I would see lights in the sky and convince myself that they were German planes, closing my eyes for a few seconds then opening them to check whether the lights had moved: they were only stars. The night sky had become a frightening place where once it had been romantic to a girl on the brink of growing up. On cloudy nights it was just as bad, for then I would lie awake listening for planes which could be hiding in the clouds and I was frightened. As the months went by my fears subsided but never really went away.

Everything was in short supply. Homes had been left fatherless and husbandless. Our menfolk were fighting against heavy odds in Europe, and life in Britain was indeed grim. A call went out nationwide for Local Defence Volunteers (LDV), later it was called the Home Guard. Hardly any of the units boasted a rifle between them and when they were issued with pikes they became a laughing stock. Some members resigned rather than carry the idiotic things, even though it was pointed out that they would be better than nothing if faced with an armed German parachutist.

In 1940 the British Expeditionary Force (BEF) retreated from occupied France and the historic evacuation from Dunkirk by the Royal Navy, the Merchant Navy and all manner of little ships took place. Norway, Holland and Belgium were overrun by Germany: Britain stood alone.

Female conscription started, women and girls had to register up to the age of fifty-one for war work. Unless they had very young children, women had to work in factories making bombs, aeroplanes, ammunition; all the things needed in war. Latchkey children were known long before mothers went to work from choice, mothers then couldn't choose. My brother and sister were still at school when our mother had to go to work at the Daimler Works in Coventry. They weren't making Daimlers then, but aeroplane engines so desperately needed. All factories worked round the clock on a shift system. Nightshift was the worst, for the long-dreaded bombing had begun. Every city was a target; Coventry's nightmare started in the autumn. Villages didn't escape altogether, for planes which didn't reach their target dropped the bombs anywhere on their way back to Germany.

I decided to join the Land Army at this time; you didn't have to be a certain age to join, but you needed parental permission.

Fancying myself behind the wheel of a tractor, though not every farm had one, I collected a form and took it home. My father refused to sign it: the work was too rough and I wasn't leaving home, he said, and that was that. Little did he know how much I would be roughing it away from home before the war was over.

Our church held weekly dances, which were attended by the Vicar sometimes, but mostly it was the Church Army Captain who officiated at the door. Ladies of the church helped him at the interval serving biscuits and lemonade. No alcoholic beverages were on offer, nor was any person allowed through the door if suspected of imbibing thereof. Once we had left school the fathers of most of us allowed their sons and daughters to attend these weekly dances held on Saturday nights. Those who wished to go, that is – not everyone did. This I found hard to understand having impatiently longed to be old enough myself. Boys who had hated Country Dancing at school and considered it cissy, now slicked down their hair with water, vaseline or whatever was needed to control unruly mops, donned best suits and sallied forth. The girls, not too sure of themselves, giggled in a cluster near the ladies' cloakroom door, an easy exit if nerves failed when invited to take the floor. The almost overnight transition from a schoolgirl wearing a gymslip to a "female fatale" was daunting for most of us. Each girl did her best to bridge the gap, subject to mother's approval, which usually meant rubbing off most of the lipstick and rouge as well as dispensing with big sister's ear rings. If big sister was not likely to be at the dance, the ear rings could be put on again in the cloakroom.

Stockings were seldom worn because of clothes rationing, so we painted our legs; chemists mixed their own unbranded leg tan which, for the inexperienced hands, was difficult to smooth evenly. Lines were drawn down the back of legs to represent fully fashioned seams. Even if you wanted to use precious coupons on stockings, they were nigh impossible to find – America had not yet come into the war, so the Yanks and nylons were not yet on the scene. Stockings then were manufactured from rayon, a yarn made from wood pulp, and some from lisle, a rather thicker yarn than rayon, made from cotton; and of course there were real silk which none of us could afford even if we saw any in the shops. School stockings were black lisle and we couldn't discard them quickly enough. Another disadvantage of painting legs was that it washed off in the rain and marked the bed sheets if you didn't wash it all off before getting into bed.

I hoped that my father would let me go to the Saturday dance but was not too optimistic about my chances. To my great joy he gave his permission. It was exciting to be going out in the evening, for up till then I had only been allowed to attend the Young People's Guild on Wednesday evenings. It was run by the Salvation Army who used a wooden building as their meeting hall in the centre of the village. The Young People's Guild welcomed all young people of any denomination and was well attended. Though it began and ended with prayers, it wasn't exactly a religious service and the tea and buns served at the end of the meeting may have resulted in larger audiences than there might have been. Some kind person or persons must have forfeited part of their rations for the tea and buns.

The fact that the dances were run by the church probably accounted for my being allowed to attend, and also the fact that everyone there knew everyone else swayed the balance in my favour. It was accepted that we all walked home together in a crowd, we didn't pair off until we were nearer eighteen. Oh yes, we had strict guidelines and not many stepped over them – the consequences could be harsh. The Drum was where the Saturday event took place: I never knew why the wooden building was called that. The dance music was live – a piano, drums, saxophone, fiddle – it could be a three piece or five. Several small bands toured the village halls with their wonderful music. All kinds of instruments appeared on the stage of The Drum at one time or another; piano accordions for the tango were popular. The young men playing in the village halls were not professional, they had other jobs, but to us young ones if they could play strict tempo then they were the best.

Parents too sometimes turned up at dances, which tended to cramp the style of their unfortunate offspring. All age groups participated and there was no lack of tutors. Elder brothers and sisters, friends' brothers and sisters, aunts, uncles and cousins.

We all learned to dance well. We learned other things too, how to mix and talk with grown-ups other than parents or teachers. As schoolchildren we had mixed socially only with our own age group; older brothers and sisters had no time for their younger encumbrances. At the Saturday dances, somehow the dividing line had vanished and we, the recent school-leavers, gained confidence with every step learned. We twirled round the floor with style, changing from gawky, twittering, nervous and shy adolescents into young ladies and gentlemen who could hold their own at social occasions without getting tongue-tied.

Once outside when the dance was over, things reverted back to "Hurry up you kids and keep all together" from elder brothers and sisters who were supposed to be home at the same time as we were, but who always had an excuse like they "helped to clear up the hall" – funny how they were always believed. We young ones learned from our elders, some learned faster than others.

Amy had been one of the unlucky ones whose father didn't approve of dancing. The man of the house was the undisputed boss, his word was law and though sometimes teenage children might rebel against seemingly unjust treatment, it was futile. Resentment smouldered though, especially if the young ones were already working and contributing to the family finances. Fathers made all decisions concerning the family and home; the whole household revolved round him. Not until you reached the age of twenty-one were you considered old enough to have a say, and not always then.

I always had Saturday evenings to look forward to while Amy, poor girl, had nothing more exciting than an evening playing Ludo and cards with a great aunt who lived with them.

On Saturday afternoons Amy and I cycled round the lanes to other villages. Often there would be something on in the church or village hall, or a notice about a forthcoming event. In summer maybe a Garden Fête, a Sale of Work, a Church Bazaar or a Harvest Tea, stalls laden with produce, homemade jams, pickles, cakes and the like. In winter maybe a Christmas Bazaar or even a concert. We could rarely afford more than a glass of lemonade or a cup of tea and a bun: nevertheless, we enjoyed it all. Village life tended to be communal, almost everyone attended whatever was going on, be it Church, Chapel, Scouts, Guides or any other organisation running things. When I saw forthcoming notices of any dances, I lost no time informing other friends who owned cycles. Permission was granted in my case if the affair was being run under the auspices of a church and if a group of us were going together. So away we'd go to seek new dancing partners, though never did we forsake The Drum; never on a Saturday night did we venture anywhere else.

By then we were confident young ladies, out of the ugly duckling stage. We had learned how to use make up with restraint and pretended an assurance we didn't all feel. However, we certainly were more at ease among strangers than when we first trod the floor, we weren't the new girls any more. Needless to say we did meet boys, young men I should say, but they were getting fewer as the weeks went by. Liaisons were made only to end before they had begun as, one by one, the young men went away to the Army, Navy and Air Force.

Sadly, those village dances, ours included, came to an end. The musicians and most of the men were gone, many of them never to return. Saddened were we all at the loss of our magic evenings, dancing to wonderful music To us it was magic. We who had never seen London spectaculars, never seen ballet or an opera, could shut out the war for a few hours in a village hall on the dance floor and think there was nowhere else better in the world to be.

Hateful, horrible Hitler; on his head we heaped all the blame and wished on him Hell and Damnation for everything, but most of all, at that time, for our loss, the Saturday dance. At one time, leaving school had meant freedom of a sort, earning your own living (well, helping to earn it), choosing your own clothes, choosing your pleasures, under parental supervision. War changed all that: there were even more restrictions and things not allowed. I regret that we young ones missed the almost carefree period of growing up between the teens and twenties. Yes, war changed many things.

I too ended up at the Daimler Works and hated every minute of it. I was still terrified of enemy planes, and the fear of being buried under tons of rubble was always with me. Volunteers were asked for in the factory to make up First Aid teams. For one hour a week (in the works' time) the teams would attend training classes and be issued with black steel helmets: these bore a white circle with a red cross in the centre and were an incentive for me to volunteer. That and the fact that I could escape for one hour a week from the great monster of a drill which I operated. I also determined to qualify and be of some use if ever I was required to be, which I fervently prayed would be never – I was no heroine. Posters had appeared on walls everywhere exhorting us to "Dig for victory" and "Waste food and feed the Hun" from the Ministry of Food (as if anyone had any to waste by that time), "Make do and mend" (we were all doing that anyway), "Women of Britain come into the factories" (again superfluous), "Walls have ears" and lots more urging us to do this or that.

Radio did its best to keep up public morale with programmes like *It's that man again* (ITMA), immensely popular from the word go. New songs were written and sung, sentimental ones of course, but the morale boosters were the ones ridiculing Hitler – all of them poking fun and reducing him from an ogre to a silly little man, wearing a silly little moustache, who had bitten off more than he could chew.

The war went on with its hardships and heartaches. Halfway though 1941 when more men were needed abroad to replace those taken prisoner, wounded or killed, Ack Ack Command found itself severely short of manpower for the defence of Britain, and General Pile suggested to the powers that be his idea, which was to train girls to take the place of men on gunsites. Much opposition ensued from certain quarters, but Winston Churchill (we had a coalition government by that time and he was Prime Minister) was in full agreement. In the autumn of that year the first (M) (i.e. mixed sex) Heavy Anti-Aircraft Battery went into action in London. Mary Churchill, a daughter of Winston Churchill, was one of the ATS. Thus, British girls were the first to take their place in a combatant role in any army in the world.

When I learned that fact I knew exactly where I wanted to be – on a gunsite. I still needed my father to sign a form, however, but this time he signed without objecting. I didn't mention guns.

Rude Awakening

February 1942 found me with a one-way ticket to Durham ATS Training Depot. The weather was dreadful – freezing winds and snow the whole time I was there. During the next few weeks of hardship, I wondered if I'd made a terrible mistake. Mistake or not, I was in for the duration and that was that.

On reflection, although I didn't think so then, the training staff at Durham did a wonderful job in four weeks to take girls from all walks of life and turn them into khaki robots. Underneath the khaki we were still very much individuals but our individuality lay dormant within the robots.

Every minute of our day was filled, much of it in queues. We queued for blankets (no sheets), information, medical inspections, hair inspections, eye tests, hearing tests, for our turn in the gas chamber with respirators on, with them off and, worst of all, for numerous injections. The further down the queue you were, the more blunt was the needle. They didn't change the needle each time, only when it wouldn't puncture skin. Of course we queued for meals. I don't remember anything about the food, but it must have been adequate to give us strength to stand in all those everlasting queues. Then again, I don't ever remember being hungry either.

Some of us slept away from the main brick building in wooden huts; rain and snow came in and there was no heating, so the minute we went into the huts at the end of our exhausting day, it was straight into bed. We had been issued with blue flannelette pyjamas and we all slept wearing our pullovers, one girl even wore a Balaclava helmet. No one in my hut whined, pride prevented that, we'd joined the army and we could take it. It seemed to be our unspoken resolve.

Discipline was absolute as, of course, it must be for any army to function, and from the first day to the last we were known only by surname. I only ever did know one girl's name, she was the one who stood in front of me in the queues. The queuing was efficient and alphabetically formed. When you reached the front, whatever or whoever was waiting for you, be it a dreaded needle or an item of kit, there was your name and file ready. Mary Struggles was the last of the Ss and I was the first of the Ts. Thomson without the P, I was always telling them.

After the first few days the lines of khaki-clad girls relaxed somewhat and chattering went on here and there. Somehow or other we two acquired the reputation of being the noisy ones and the NCO in charge would shout in tones which certainly weren't dulcet. "Struggles and Thomson, less noise down there!" and it wasn't always us. No other names were ever called out as far as I remember, it seemed that the linked names had a menacing ring which they could easily remember; perhaps they did this with each new intake, picked on two names. Well we could put up with that if we were only being shouted at we said to each other. Struggles was noisy and brash I thought, she was always cheerful and nothing dismayed her or worried her. She was small (we were actually the same size), blonde and bubbly, pretty, blue eyes, fair skin, wide smile. That description fitted me with exceptions, take away bubbly, wide smile except on occasions and change pretty into passable. The others called us the Terrible Twins. At first I didn't like Struggles at all, she reminded me of a puppy round your feet always wanting your attention and not giving in until she got it. Irritating most of the time, but as we spent so long in close proximity, gradually my reserve melted and I could see she had more good points than bad. It wouldn't hurt me to adopt some of them I thought, so eventually I earned the reputation of being one half of a noisy pair. We became friends, she wasn't sleeping in my hut which was a good thing; the rest of my hut-mates were quiet and serious. It was a serious business this training – odd how we had all landed in the same hut, they couldn't have known our characters on the first day, surely? Struggles told me one day that she had been determined to make me like her and she said it put her back up when I didn't respond to her.

"You were so damn serious I thought you must be a vicar's daughter or something," she said.

"Obviously you haven't met many daughters of vicars," I retorted somewhat sharply.

She laughed and said "Now now, don't get uppish again."

"Was I really as bad as that?" I asked.

"Yes but you're improving," she answered.

Another girl in the Ts said "It's enough to change everyone's character in here, it's like being in prison except we volunteered and didn't get dragged in screaming, no we just walked in like lambs to the slaughter."

"Do you think if we scream loud enough they'll let us out?" said Struggles.

"Well we're only here for a month, surely we're not going to spend the whole time queuing?" I said.

"What do you know about prison?" said Struggles "Have you been in prison then?"

"Yes I have" was the reply, "I visited my brother in prison." "Go on, go on!" urged Struggles, "What had he done?"

"It's what he hadn't done, he refused to pay maintenance to his wife – said he would go to prison rather than pay that slut of a wife one penny. He is serving three months in a prison near Leicester."

Struggles wanted more, "Go on," but I interrupted.

"Didn't he have to pay the debt when he came out?"

"No the prison sentence cancels out the debt, but the day he is released from prison it starts adding up again so I don't know what will happen."

Struggles burst in impatiently, "What brought it all on, I'm dying to know, why did he call his wife a slut?"

"Well you'll just have to die then, I don't want to talk about it any more," said the other.

"Well," Struggles went on unabashed, "surely prison is a lot worse than this place? We don't have iron cages and warders with great bunches of rattling keys."

By this time others were listening, one said with a grin, "You've been watching too many Yankee films."

Then the usual roar, "Struggles and Thomson, this is your last warning!" and silence reigned for the remainder of that particular queuing session. Struggles never did find out about that slut of a wife.

We were taught to march by a male sergeant (Sergeant) who marched us until our feet were blistered: I already had chilblains. The new army shoes were heavier than we were used to, not really good enough for learning how to march when all we had done in them was shuffle along in queues. Apart from the discomfort, I quite enjoyed drill, it felt good to move as one body, each pair of feet doing exactly the same. This didn't happen overnight of course, but when everyone remembered which was their right foot and which was their left, things improved rapidly. We must have been good although I never heard the instructor say so, but he took us out marching in the streets of Durham and I don't think he would have risked his own reputation if we hadn't been passable.

One day we were out marching near the river when it started to snow. The Sergeant halted us, told us to "Fall Out", then ordered us to descend a flight of perilous looking steps to the riverside. To our surprise he then led us into a cosy tea room with steamed-up windows where we spent a pleasant hour scoffing tea and buns, at our own expense of course.

When the Sergeant decided it was time to go he said, "Listen you lot, you haven't been here, it was just a dream, got that?"

"Yes Sergeant!" we chorused as one.

I wondered for ages afterwards just how that tea room came to be open in midwinter. That February day I was only thankful that it was.

We obeyed all orders, accepted all happenings without question. I don't remember having an evening pass to leave the depot or indeed any free time in the evenings. If we did, then I must have been too exhausted to take advantage of it. Eventually, we did other things besides queue: we were offered a choice of careers, and naturally I chose Anti-Aircraft Defence. After girls had chosen a career from the list, they were then assessed as to their suitability for it. Then there were all kinds of tests to go through, for Ack Ack anyway. We had to spot aircraft on film – sounds easy but wasn't – there were tests to check for steadiness of hand, accuracy of eye and hand, questions galore till I was sure that I wouldn't pass. To my great relief I did; it was like gaining an honours degree when I was accepted for Anti-Aircraft Defence training and was only the second bright moment during that four weeks. I don't remember very much laughter, we hadn't learned how to mix grumbles with a joke, it was all so serious.

There were muffled sobs sometimes after Lights Out and I have to admit that some were mine, not one of us crept out to comfort another. We all felt I'm sure, that no one but ourselves was the prime cause of us being there at all and we weren't going to admit that we couldn't take it. Each of us respected the others' private misgivings. All the time that I spent in uniform I've never ever been as miserable as I was that first month, nothing was ever quite so bad again.

Royal Artillery Barracks

On a cold windy day in March, our batch of trainees departed from Durham, not having seen much of that city. Struggles, myself and two others were *en route* for the Royal Artillery Barracks at Arborfield and the rest to wherever they were to receive training. The two other girls I didn't really know: although Stevenson had been in the S queue, she hadn't been at the noisy end. I don't remember the name of the other girl and didn't get to know her because she was sent back for re-training before the period at Arborfield ended.

We were met at Wokingham railway station and transported to the Barracks in an army truck. Collected by an ATS corporal we were led to the stores to pick up blankets and pillows. Our sleeping quarters were to be in a large barrack room with two-tier bunks. On each of them lay three biscuits – army biscuits were not the edible kind but square pads filled with straw, which served as a mattress. The beds looked decidedly rickety and were. Somehow I ended up with a top bunk, Struggles sitting on a bottom one and saying, "This one's mine." Nearly all the beds were made up, Stevenson and the other girl therefore had to look for vacant beds at the other end of the room. All this time the corporal had barked the information at us, but of course we were used to that. She told us about the evening meal and the time of reveille, what time to parade for breakfast then, thankfully, departed.

Struggles for once was quiet. She looked round the room; some girls were unpacking, others sitting on beds writing letters, a few were talking among themselves. I supposed that they knew each other from the Initial Training camp. We had, it seemed, come from all over the British Isles by the sound of the different dialects.

"Well," I ventured, "we had better make our beds, come on, stop dreaming."

Struggles said, getting up, "I'm not dreaming, I'm thinking. I wonder if we can go out tonight?"

"Out, out where?" I queried.

"Just out," she said, "out of the camp. If I don't get out soon, I'll forget what it's like."

"OK then, we'll find out when we go for our meal, but now I'm going to try and make this bed. I think the best plan is to help each other, it will be simpler," and I climbed up on the top bunk. It swayed and creaked – really it was only four posts fastened together with two wire mesh platforms which, when covered by three biscuits and blankets, was a bed. Each time the one on the top moved, the whole thing swayed. I could do with sea-sickness pills, I thought, and said so. Struggles had found her giggle and it bubbled, the thought of our possible outing had brought it forth. The beds were all the same, definitely First War vintage we decided.

It appeared that no one knew of any reason why we shouldn't go out of camp that first night; we were duly warned of the time to report in at the Guardroom and the time of Lights Out. Back in the barrack room I quickly found my Brasso and shoe polish, cleaned buttons, cap, badge and shoes; took towel, soap, toothbrush and make-up to the ablutions (washroom) and proceeded to try to make myself look, if not exactly glamorous, as near to it as I could. Surveying myself in the mirror, as much as I could see (which wasn't much, it being fixed high enough for soldiers when shaving), I decided that I had done all I could to improve on nature and returned to the barrack room.

It was then I found out that Struggles had a serious flaw in her character. Never having had the opportunity to discover this, not having planned an outing before, it was an unpleasant surprise for me. I who could get ready as quick as a flash and be off, had now to sit and wait and wait! Struggles making up her face was something to watch if you had nothing better to do. I, who had better things to do, was trying to keep my blood pressure down and my temper cool. Asking how much longer it would be before she was ready was useless, after the third time of asking I gave up, her answer was always "In a minute." I looked at the time every few minutes, walked to the ablutions and back twice, looked round at the other girls in various stages of undress, some already in the army-issue blue flannelette stripes.

We two seemed to be the only ones with any intention of leaving quarters till reveille, that is if we ever did. Perhaps their initial training had not been as rigorous or regimented as ours, perhaps they had enjoyed evenings out during the previous month's training or maybe they were just re-charging their batteries for the unknown tomorrow. A month's semi-incarceration in Durham had made us eager for a taste of freedom, though you wouldn't have thought so, the time she was taking. Left to myself I think I would have opted for an early night and some letter writing, but when Struggles suggested going out, I was as keen as she was. At last, with a final look in the mirror perched on her doubled up pillow, she was ready. I refrained with difficulty from remarking that we wouldn't have time to get far before it was time to come back. In silence we made our way towards the gate and had not gone more than a few yards when we were stopped by the same corporal who had welcomed us!

"Where are you two going?" she barked.

"We are allowed out aren't we?" said Struggles.

"Yes but where are you going? There's nowhere to go." snapped the corporal.

She is probably right, I thought. On the way from the station it had seemed a fair way to the Barracks and there didn't seem much of a village.

Struggles answered brightly, "We thought we'd find a dance somewhere, do you know if there is one?"

"There is a dance here tomorrow night at the gym," was the reply and she glared at us. "What are your names again?"

"Private Struggles, and where is the NAAFI then?"

"And your name?" I gave mine meekly, thinking she will remember the two of us from now on. She glared again and gave us directions to the NAAFI, then walked off towards the gate.

"I wonder where she's off to? We're not giving up are we?"

"No blooming fear," I said, "not after I've waited all this time for you to get ready! We'll ask the sentry on duty if he knows where the nearest dance is, or at least when and where they do have dances. We are going outside this gate even if it's only for a walk!"

The sentry was most helpful, he told us that it was a fair bit of a walk, but the California Club had dancing most nights. The quickest way on foot, he said, was to strike off the main road where the woods began and over the stile, follow the path alongside a fence keeping the woods on our right. "Keep going," he went on "until you come to a clearing between the trees, that will be the car park at the back of the building. You'll see the vehicles, or should if you've been eating plenty of carrots." It was believed then that carrots, if you ate enough of them, would enable you to see better in the dark. Rumour had it that the RAF encouraged pilots to consume large quantities. Struggles listened to these precise instructions with dismay.

"We'll never find it!" she said.

"You shouldn't be in the army then," retorted the sentry.

Struggles was a city girl from Birmingham and, though used to the blackout, she said that at least you could identify shapes in the streets there. The countryside that night appeared to be a solid blackness with no glimmer of light. "Come on," I urged, "who was it who wanted to see the great wide world outside? Your eyes will soon adjust to the dark and it will do us good to do something on our own initiative." She still looked doubtful. "I wish we had a torch."

"Well we haven't so come on!" I said, going underneath the barrier: she followed.

"Good luck and don't forget the way back!" shouted the sentry.

We set off along the road, walking on the grass verge when we heard any traffic approaching, watching for the dense blackness that would mean the woods. It wasn't far that bit; we found the stile, climbed over it and felt for the fence. The path

was a bit rough but on we went, stumbling sometimes over
roots, holding on to the fence at times, till we reached the car
park. We felt our way round cars and trucks in search of the
entrance. Struggles cheered up as we heard music, dance music.

"I hope the Ladies is near the door," she said, "I bet we look
like the babes in the wood covered with half a forest." It was
true we had gathered a few bits of foliage; parts of the path had
been rather overgrown. The main drive seemed to be round the
other side and we edged carefully along the wall feeling for the
entrance. Once inside we made a beeline for the Ladies, shook
our uniforms free of twigs and leaves and looked round the
very "posh" Ladies Room. Mirrors galore, a wine coloured
carpet with curtains to match, a row of velvet-covered stools
sat beneath a shelf, each one had a mirror; luxury indeed! I
remember it so well for it was the smartest Ladies Room I had
ever used. Struggles sat down on one of the stools. Strains of
music could be heard. "If you think I'm waiting for you, you're
wrong," I said to her reflection in the mirror. "You'll do." She
patted a curl and jumped up, I was halfway through the door.
No lack of partners – almost immediately we were both
whirled onto the dance floor: it was heavenly. I had never seen
as many musicians on a stage before, professional musicians.
Oh, it had been worth the woodland walk. Struggles and I
were partnered for every dance; nearly all the men were in
uniform, a few wore civilian suits, but there were hardly any
girls in uniform.

Struggles too was impressed with the California Country
Club even though she told me that Birmingham had places to
equal it. I had certainly never been inside such a place and
intended to visit again if the chance arose. With that in mind I
kept my eye on the time, knowing we would have to leave ages
before the dance ended to be sure of getting back in time.
Having found this wonderful place it would be too bad if we
ended up being confined to Barracks for part or all of the month
we were to spend at Arborfield. My partner twirled me into a
graceful spin at the end of a dreamy waltz. As the lights went up
I found myself looking over his shoulder at another ATS
uniform and the face looking over her partner's shoulder at me
was the face of the barking corporal! She didn't smile.

I nearly ran from my partner in my haste to impart this discovery to Struggles.

"Well!" she exclaimed, "the crafty cat, I bet she wonders how we got here, do you think she'll say anything?"

"There's nothing she can say is there? she didn't exactly tell us a lie but it was mean of her all the same," I answered. Struggles giggled saying "Well that shows that she is afraid of competition, as we're both blonde and ours didn't come out of a bottle. I bet hers did!"

Two smart young men asked us for the next dance. I didn't recognise the uniform – it was navy blue with a red stripe down the trousers, buttoned up to the neck and on the shoulders, silver mesh epaulettes. It turned out that they were bandsmen from a Military Cadet Band School nearby. They invited us to a dance being held at the school the following week and of course we accepted with pleasure, especially as they were both excellent dancers. The two were about our own age, but we met some boys much younger when, the following week, we were guests at the Band School and they all danced. The younger boys though were not allowed to go to outside dances. Tea and soft drinks, fruit cake and sandwiches were served at the interval. I enjoyed that part of the evening almost as much as the dancing. It was nothing like the California, but the music was every bit as good, naturally. Again, not many girls in uniform and although a fair number of girls were guests, the boys outnumbered them. We had partners of various ages, some just learning to dance and some who would never be dancers; there was a nice atmosphere though and it was fun.

Of course we visited the California again as often as we were able and enjoyed more waltzes and quicksteps with our two cadets. As on that first visit we made sure we arrived back on time. The ATS corporal never ever mentioned seeing us and of course we kept quiet. Always having to leave before a dance ended, never being able to have the last waltz, was a deprivation we suffered all through our army career. We hardly ever had the chance to be escorted home, for it was usually during the last waltz the male dancers swarmed the floor hoping to escort a girl home. Later on in our service lives we'd be granted Twenty-four

Hour Passes and maybe a rare Late Pass when we did have the pleasure of dancing the last waltz.

I would be dancing on a variety of dance floors during the war years, from ballrooms with sprung floors to little tin canteen huts and numerous village and church halls. From famous bands to just a piano and drums, but Joe Loss, Oscar Rabin, Nat Gonella and many others of that era were pleasures yet to unfold. At that time the California Country Club was all I knew of the high life and the walk through the woods, come wind come weather, was nothing.

A bugle sounded reveille, after all I was in a Royal Artillery Barracks. Some of my room mates were not sure what it was, but they soon found out it meant getting up. I thrilled to its sound that first morning; for me it was proof that I was actually in the army. Many a morning afterwards, thrilled was not the word I used. However, that morning, everything was exciting and I looked forward with eagerness to the day ahead. The fact that I had located somewhere to spend a few pleasant hours in my free time played no small part in the zest for life at that early hour.

After breakfast we paraded in two squads, ATS and soldiers of the Royal Artillery. To me the men looked old, at my age everyone older than thirty seemed old. Names were read out, men and girls formed into four mixed sections and were marched away in different directions. Our section ended up outside a lecture hut and was ordered to Halt and Fall Out. Inside, like a schoolroom, were a blackboard and rows of tables and chairs. The ATS wearing skirts and shoes, the men dressed in battledress and heavy boots, clattered on the bare wooden floor; each one sitting on a chair beside another of the same gender – the men not looking directly at the girls but sneaking glances as they sat down. Just as the last few had seated themselves we heard "Section Section 'Shun" and in a flurry of movement we did ''Shun' but the sound was not unlike machine-gun-fire. I sincerely hoped that it would sound better the next time, surely it wasn't only we four from Durham who had been taught army drill? A young earnest looking 2nd Lieutenant strode in accompanied by the Sergeant who had marched us there. The Sergeant gave the order to Stand at Ease and Stand Easy and we sat down again.

Lieutenant Revill addressed his troops. He wasn't at all happy to be in charge of a mixed section of gunners, he told us, but he would have to accept the fact that we were his section and so would we. C Section 536 (m), Heavy Anti-Aircraft Battery of the Royal Artillery, that was us. He went on to tell us that a battery (for the benefit of the ATS) consisted of four sections which would man two gunsites, one of them would be Headquarters (HQ). When we had completed our training, the Battery would be posted to defend an airfield, dockyard, arms depot, or some other important establishment from the air. Each site would be manned by four 3.7 guns with maybe smaller Lewis guns or Bofors as well.

Ack Ack required a fair standard of intelligence as well as powers of endurance and we would have to suffer public abuse when we failed to shoot down every German aircraft in sight. He went on to tell us that the two weapons in the air defence of Britain were Fighter Command and Ack Ack Command, which would be in close liaison with the nearest Fighter Group, the right hand having to know what the left hand was doing. Although the guns must always be ready and waiting for targets, sometimes they would need to hold fire because of RAF proximity. The battery would have to maintain a high standard of training and share none of the glory of Fighter Command.

Standing there so smartly, several times nervously clearing his throat, tapping his cane to emphasise a point, he had everyone's undivided attention. He told us what to expect and what he expected of us. The strictest Fire discipline must be observed at all times, whether it was practice or not. He said the gunners were to treat the ATS as equals in everything, that we each had a job to do regardless of sex. Winning the war was all that mattered and our job was to defend Britain from the air. He ended by saying we must live and work together with that one aim and possibly, quite possibly, to die together.

We all went away from that lecture room subdued but inspired. He had lit a spark among us (the ATS anyway), but whether he ever realised it I don't know. He had given us equal status as gunners alongside men and we were determined to prove that we were capable of all he expected of us. I have never forgotten, and never will, that first day at Arborfield, that first assembly as part of a real operational unit. I told myself I wasn't a robot any more, but an individual and part of a team. I had learned at school how important the team spirit was, but this was more demanding than a school hockey or netball team. From that day C Section would have to weld itself into a formidable weapon.

James Revill, 2nd Lieutenant (we called him Jimmy among ourselves) was, his batman told us, the best officer in the Battery and we should be the best section in the Battery for that reason. A year or so later Jimmy was posted, but not before he had licked us into shape as gunners. He instilled in us a pride in our Command Post drill, which we carried out efficiently, whether it was practice or the real thing. The competitive spirit between men and girls developed and was the main reason for the high standard at all times.

After dinner that first day the section marched to the gun park. Of course to the men it was a familiar sight, but for us who had never even seen a picture of an anti-aircraft gun, it was a little overwhelming to be confronted all at once with our weapons of war.

To my dismay I discovered that the next four weeks, while being trained on the instruments, if any of us didn't reach the standard required, we would be sent back to be re-trained for something else. This did happen to some: I dreaded it happening to me. We really worked hard; as always when you are being tried and tested, you seem to have a driving force that keeps you on your toes the whole time and always at the back of your mind is the fear of failure. We had all volunteered for Ack Ack and didn't want to do anything else, so it mattered very much that we passed on all counts; enthusiasm wasn't quite enough.

Every day we trained as teams, with instruments and guns. Spotters picked up the target with binoculars, they also had a small telescope. Height finder and Predictor also had telescopes and, directed by the spotters, they lined up the target. The Height finder team would adjust images on the double-vision screen and follow the target manually, transmitting certain information to the Predictor, height and so on. The Predictor, on receiving the information would predict precisely where the target would be when the guns fired. All this needed the steady hands and eyes of the teams, as manually they had to match moving dials steadily and accurately, wind speeds, bearing range, etc. This information was carried to the guns nearby. Electrical impulses passed through cables along the ground to dials on the guns. Radar was as yet still in its infancy and not many sets were in use. It was by telephone that spotters were informed of the probable direction of enemy aircraft. Spotters were on duty scanning the skies all the hours of daylight and telephones were manned the whole time.

Gradually the equipment was modified, all though the war years improvements were made. Even so, all sites were not equipped with the latest sophistications. One from each team would attend a course to learn how to operate the newer systems as they came off the drawing board.

The whole section trained together on the gun park. Of course there was more than one team for each instrument and gun, the ones who weren't actually manning a gun or an instrument sat on wobbly benches. Woe betide you if you let your attention wander for an instant from the team who were operating the instrument, or the instructor! The instructors were male and, because they didn't appear to approve of girl gunners either, they didn't miss an opportunity to catch out anyone who wasn't paying attention. Ours would point to a girl, "You there, what is Number Three doing?" or "What was my last command?" We soon realised that he could see through the back of his head and were careful not to look around at what may be happening on the guns or the Height finder. It was in our interest to note all that he said and not miss a word. We were keen to master the intricacies of the instrument anyway, to prove to ourselves and our officers that we could be as efficient as the men. I was a Predictor number, on the gun park we were known by numbers. Naturally, working with the Predictor was a lot more interesting than sitting watching and when Number One shouted, "On Target," everything hummed into action, dials lit up, handles spinning to put in wind correction and fuse settings: concentration was intense as each operator watched her own dial and obeyed the signals.

On the large barrack square we had marching drill in sections with the men. There was a vast difference between marching with a squad of ATS at Durham being drilled by a clear-dictioned male Sergeant and marching on a large barrack square with two or three other squads being drilled at one and the same time, each with a regular army Sergeant who stood a long distance from his squad. It took quite a while to identify your own instructor's voice and even longer to decipher his commands, which when barked across a large area on a windy day, sounded nothing like "Section will move to the right in threes" or "About turn." I could distinguish the command "Halt" but not always which instructor was giving it. However, after a few mix-ups with other sections intermingling, we all got sorted out and did as well as any other battery which had been on the Arborfield square, I suppose. We had to pass in everything, not just on the gun park, and according to the drill Sergeant if we could march well, we could do anything. Later, on site, the ATS Sergeants were every bit as good as their male counterparts, I particularly enjoyed the drill where commands were given simultaneously.

While the other sections were on the gun park, our section would be in a lecture room. We had lectures on Army Discipline, Security, Defence, and hardest of all for me was Aircraft Recognition. Apart from the bi-planes, to me they all looked the same; but gradually, after watching lots of training films, studying diagrams and photographs as well as having to draw them, I did eventually learn to see the difference and could tell a German plane from a British one. Somehow the German planes looked ugly, their names seemed threatening, Junkers, Heinkels, Dorniers, Stukas and Messerschmitts. The man who taught us Aircraft Recognition used a blackboard to draw the parts of aircraft and his hands a lot to demonstrate the wings. We had to learn the silhouette of each aircraft and he used the word dihedral so often that we nicknamed him Dihedral Joe.

One sunny day my section was in the lecture room and I was in a seat next to a window, the sun felt warm through the glass, the window was high, but I could see the tops of the trees, they were just coming in to leaf. I felt a wave of homesickness, it seemed a long time since I had walked or cycled the lanes of Warwickshire. The Predictor Instructor who was taking the session had a very soft voice. He was Polish, but with only the trace of an accent and he could be so sarcastic on occasions. I had felt the flush of embarrassment a few times from his barbs. It was pleasantly warm in the room even though a cold wind was blowing outside, shaking the trees. His voice went on, I heard the voice, but was not listening to the words, I was walking the woods at home. Then I heard my name, "Private Thomson" and was suddenly jerked back from my wanderings to find all eyes on me. "Now that we have Private Thomson with us again," the velvety voice went on, "maybe she can answer my last question?" Of course I couldn't, I hadn't even heard it. My face was hot and not because of the warmth of the room. I blushed easily, it was such a giveaway; I could never pretend a nonchalance I didn't feel and how I hated him at that moment, that man! He carried on with a few more clever and cutting remarks before going on with the lecture. I smarted for the rest of the day, I felt that I had let the ATS down, especially knowing what he thought of us as gunners. Even though we were supposed to have the title, on the gun park he always addressed us by whatever number we were on the instrument. I suppose in his opinion we had to earn the title Gunner before he would use it, not that he ever did. However, he was a good instructor and taught well. It was up to him who passed for Ack Ack and who didn't, so we all strove our utmost to avoid being on the receiving end of his biting remarks, which could shrivel you up. Needless to say, I didn't do any more woolgathering when he was in charge and my hatred for him faded. Afterwards, when we talked among ourselves about him, we realised that, for all the instructors in the Royal Artillery, it must be a daunting thought to know the responsibility for Britain's defence lay on their shoulders. To take girls who had only been in uniform a month, had never seen a big gun, and in four weeks train them to be competent on gun controlling instruments relaying vital data to guns was asking a lot.

Comrades in Arms

In the large well-equipped gymnasium we did Physical Training (PT). Ropes, bars and "horses" to vault over, or for the not so agile, to crawl over. I think most of us enjoyed PT in the gym much more than on site when we did it out of doors in all kinds of weather, summer and winter. The floor of the gym turned into a dance floor once a week – there we did dance the last waltz, for that took place well before Lights Out.

Although our days were full and more interesting than the previous month had been, our evenings were free. There was the NAAFI canteen and we were allowed evening passes. There was homework to do, notes to revise, Aircraft Recognition books to study and aircraft to draw. I wasn't very good at that, but as we became more sure of ourselves, we relaxed a little and looked forward to visiting the California Club. At least some of us did, for we discovered others also loved dancing, so the pathway was well trodden through the woods.

Struggles and I found ourselves in different sections, so we didn't see each other during the day except at mealtimes, but our friendship continued. Still getting the blame for things like talking after Lights Out – I suppose records were in our files from Durham. Meals at Arborfield tended to be repetitive, rissoles three times a week and square, individual apple pies several times a week. These were sold in the NAAFI too, in packets with a brand name so the army cooks didn't bake apple pies.

At some time during the four weeks each one of us was granted a twenty-four-hour pass. Not everyone could reach their homes and back in that short space of time, so some slept in barracks. Struggles and I decided at once to go straight to London, neither of us had been before and we agreed that now was the time while there still was a city to visit. Typical of the sheer folly of youth, or optimism, whichever way you look at it, we were headed as fast as our legs could carry us towards Hitler's prime bombing target. If we'd been killed in an air raid, our training would all have counted for naught. Our guardian angels were with us that time and we both returned unscathed to complete our training. We found out that a bus service operated from Reading to London. I don't remember how we got to Reading, but I will always remember that journey to London as being one of the most uncomfortable journeys I have ever experienced, even counting the ones on troop trains, army trucks and, once, sitting on top of a pile of ammunition on the back of a lorry in the middle of an air raid.

The driver let everyone who was waiting board the bus, it was an accepted thing in wartime, though unofficial. That London-bound bus however, did well to reach its destination without breaking down. If the proverbial sardines had been packed in as we were, they would have ended up as mash. The conductor collected fares as each person got off the bus.

On reaching the terminus, we asked the way to the Young Women's Christian Association hostel (YWCA) and set forth. After getting lost once, a very easy thing to do, we reached the hostel only to be told they were full up for the night. We were given directions to a Catholic Women's hostel, luckily not far away, and thankfully were allocated a bed each in a dormitory there. While signing in we were offered free tickets to a dance being held at the Canadian Forces club that evening. Fortune favours the brave: I thought, what luck, yes please and thank you. Clutching the tickets I followed the Fairy Godmother along the corridor with Struggles following me. I hadn't heard a giggle from that young lady for quite some time, but she giggled when we reached the dormitory. After telling us where the bathroom was, where breakfast would be served, the time it would be served and the time the door would be locked that night, the Fairy Godmother left us. Struggles collapsed on one of the beds in near hysterics. I never knew half the time the reason for her merriment. We really were complete opposites, I was a sobersides compared to her and took life seriously most of the time. She sat up, "We're here," she said, "in uniform, learning how to defend the likes of her with guns and she treats us like schoolgirls. This is just how I imagine it must be at boarding school. Look at it, all these curtains separating the beds, they might just as well have saved their coupons. What difference do curtains make? Are they supposed to make it more private?"

The room was empty apart from us, all the other occupants foraging for food no doubt, it being early evening by this time. "Oh come on Struggles" I answered, "Let's go and eat, this place only serves breakfast. Oh no! you are not going to do your face before we eat are you? Wait till we go to the dance." She was delving into her make-up bag. "I'll just do my lips." Resignedly I walked over to look out of the window. The lengthy make-up sessions never ceased to infuriate me, nothing I said made any difference. Struggles would calmly go on doing what she wanted to do and cheerfully dismissed my threats with a laugh. Funny how she always just managed to make the parades on time, only just. Without appearing to hurry she could slide into place as if she had just strolled there.

The evening did not turn out as exciting as we had anticipated, for the uniformed British Servicewomen were greatly outnumbered by the civilian girls. In their pretty dresses with long glamorous hairstyles, they outshone the drab khaki-and airforce-blue-clad ones, however shiny their buttons and shoes. The Canadians seemed to want to get away from uniforms. Another thing, shapely legs did not look their best when encased in thick lisle stockings and heavy flat shoes. To our utter chagrin we sat out more than we danced, this lack of partners had never happened to us before. After a few soft drinks at the bar we decided that we'd had enough, we wouldn't stay there to be ignored. Actually that wasn't strictly true, we had been chatted up at the bar, for there were plenty of unaccompanied Canadians but they all turned out to be non-dancers and, charming as they may have been, we were only interested in dancing. So refusing all offers of various categories except dancing, we excused ourselves and went in the direction of the Ladies' cloakroom, then departed for an early night. Of course we hadn't said we were intent on leaving the club in case we were followed by any of them who didn't seem to understand the word no. Fancy, going home early from a dance on a 24-hr pass at that and in London! We weren't going back to Barracks to crow of our wonderful night out in London, that was certain. In any case we told each other, if we had been enjoying ourselves, we should still have had to leave before the dance ended as the hostel door was locked at 11 p.m. and there was always tomorrow.

It turned out that there wasn't much time on the morrow for we had to be on parade at 2.30 p.m. Luckily though we found the shop we wanted, the Army and Navy Stores, and there we bought white lanyards, RA grenade badges which we were allowed to wear as gunners, and officers' ties which we weren't, then it was time to head back for the bus to Reading. Before leaving the shop we proudly fastened the white lanyards on right shoulders, marching along proudly wearing the gunners' lanyards, saluting every British officer in sight and receiving salutes in return. We felt as important as a couple of Generals. Five minutes later we were stopped by the dreaded Redcaps (ATS Military Police) who told us we were improperly dressed, that the ATS lanyard was in the ATS colours of orange and brown and to take off the white ones immediately. Indignantly we protested that we were indeed properly dressed and that we were part of Ack Ack Command, therefore entitled as gunners to wear the white lanyard. In vain, the Redcaps, their education sadly lacking about the ATS they were policing, insisted that we remove the offending lanyards or else. The two of us stood there in the middle of London, smarting with humiliation and simmering with fury at their ignorance. With discretion being the better of valour, we removed the lanyards in front of all who were watching.

The minute we boarded the bus we promptly put them on again, needing something to soothe our deflated egos. We were understandably quiet for a while looking out of the bus windows at the bomb-damaged streets, then Struggles turned to me and without the glimmer of a smile said, "Was our journey really necessary?" Well that set us off, we both started giggling, the kind you can't stop, trying to laugh quietly but the more we tried to subdue it, the worse it got. I'm sure the other passengers must have thought we were crazy. It didn't sound as funny when related to the others later that day, but the two of us often laughed about it.

An unusual event took place one day; the ATS were told to parade after the morning break for Rifle Practice. With some trepidation therefore, mixed with pride that someone actually considered us capable enough to handle a rifle, we awaited the whistle for parade. Most of us, not yet twenty-one and under legal age for doing almost anything, were to be handed a rifle with ammunition. It was one thing to be part of a team feeding a gun with data for firing, where someone else was in command and quite another to be in sole charge of a lethal weapon and responsible for its destructive power. As we marched to the Armoury I was first filled with apprehension, then cold fear that I would not do as well as the others. Not that I might hit someone by mistake, as one girl confessed afterwards she had been scared of doing. The instructors taught us how to use the "pull through" and load the rifle. I don't know how many trembling fingers there were among us that day but ten of them were mine. Ours happened to be the first section for this new venture. I wondered what Struggles would find to joke about when Section D marched to the Armoury. It had certainly been sprung upon us, no one up to that minute before morning break had ever mentioned anything about ATS being armed.

We were shown how to position our bodies on the ground, with sandbags to assist the aim. Instructors walked along the line of marksmen, kicking feet into the correct angle. There were a number of targets and the appropriate number of girls on the ground, the rest looking on. When the instructor was satisfied that each girl was correctly aligned and each knew which target she should be aiming for, he gave the order to take aim then roared, "Fire!" To everyone's amazement and relief we all hit the target, though some of us only just caught the edge.

We each had six shots – although we had been warned of the thump on the shoulder when the trigger was pulled, it took me by surprise. However, no one disgraced C Section and the others took their turn on the ground. I do wish there had been a camera to record that memorable occasion, as watching from behind, each one of them looked every inch a soldier wearing battledress, boots and gaiters, rifles at the ready. By that time we had been issued with boots, socks, gaiters and battledress. Considering that none of the ATS had ever used a rifle before, to deliver them into our hands and allow us to fire them with only a brief introduction to the art showed courage indeed, worthy of a medal, I considered, to whichever officer had ordered the exercise. I'd be willing to bet that it wasn't one of our own officers.

Our glory was short-lived for that was the only time we handled a rifle in our army career. No other section marched to the Armoury. We never did find out why and it worried us all until we were told unofficially that it was not because we had done badly on the Firing Range, far from it. We had to be content with that, but all of us without exception would have welcomed an opportunity to thank whoever it was for his faith in the ATS. Even if some of us were relieved to know that Rifle Practice was not going to be part of our curriculum.

As well as being issued with battledress, we had acquired a leather jerkin, steel helmet, knife, fork, spoon, enamel mug, rubber groundsheet, gas cape and long johns, which for some reason we had to hand back to stores, a pity for we were in need of the long johns in winters on gunsite. The khaki groundsheet did duty as a raincoat – it had cords which fastened round the neck – not an elegant garment with corners hanging. The gas cape covered the body from neck to foot and was supposedly camouflaged with brown and yellow splodges. When carried, it rolled into a neat shape fastened on the back of the neck so that when needed, a string was pulled and the cape covered the body, thereby protecting the wearer from liquid-gas attack. If ordered to march in full uniform, for the ATS gunners it meant battledress, boots, gaiters, greatcoats, steel helmet, gas cape and respirator fastened on the chest. Sometimes dressed in that way, we were ordered when marching to "double" – that meant running.

Before going to Firing Camp we needed to be fully kitted out. I don't know how long the "Soldier's Housewife" has been part of a soldier's kit, but the ATS were also issued with one of these. It was a calico strip with darning needles and darning wool, with tapes to tie round it and was pronounced "Hussif". Once we had the full Ack Ack kit including a pair of mess tins, which we didn't discover a use for until much later, we were taught how to lay out every piece of clothing and equipment on a bed. From then on Kit Inspections were a regular part of our lives. Every item had to be accounted for, whether you were wearing it or it was at the laundry.

As (m) HAA was still fairly recent, all the instructors were regular soldiers and would eventually be needed abroad, so ATS instructors were being taught to eventually take over. One day I was sent for by a Staff Officer and asked if I would volunteer to stay at Arborfield to be an instructor, it would mean instant promotion and of course more pay. I was given a few hours to decide. To say I was surprised was putting it mildly, but when I recovered from the unexpected request, I didn't need time to think about it, I knew. I was staying in C Section 536 (m) HAA Bty RA. Let whoever wanted be an instructor, I wanted to be a gunner.

As the weeks went by, each section seemed to move in, as it were, and although in the barrack room it was still the same hotchpotch from all the different Basic Training Camps, (girls from all over Britain), there was a difference. Each girl identified with her own section and drew away a little from the rest, there was a competitive atmosphere. Without realising it we were bonding each section into a whole. Things were changing from "me" and "mine" to "our section" and later at Firing Camp where other batteries were training also, it was "our battery" and "the other battery".

Struggles and I inevitably were drawing apart, we went dancing of course the two of us, and still had great fun. Whether that Corporal had anything to do with us being put into different sections I don't know, but I wondered. During the month at Arborfield, she and some of the other Corporals were made up to Sergeants. Fortunately for me, I was not in her section, nor was Struggles, but she was unfortunate enough to be in one of the two sections destined to be HQ Site after our training at Firing Camp. This fact of course was not known to us till much later on, we never learned about any army matters beforehand.

We woke up to the sound of the bugle for the last time in Aborfield Barracks, it was our last day. After 2 p.m. parade we found ourselves with some free time, unexpected but very welcome. Because the battery was not moving out till evening and because we were in battledress ready for the move out, permission was not granted for the ATS to go on a bus to town. We did get permission to go for a walk, otherwise we were supposed to keep out of sight in a barrack room or somewhere till tea parade. It was a lovely sunny day; Struggles, myself and four others from our room decided that we would like to see the California Club in daylight. In the NAAFI at dinner-time we had bought chocolate, the non-smokers would swop cigarette coupons for sweet coupons, this worked very well and pleased both parties. The six of us walked out of the gate along the road to the stile and into the woods a little way. Always before, we had stuck to the path on the way to and from the dance, but the woods looked so different in the bright spring sunshine, we were tempted to delve further. It was so overgrown, however, that damage to uniforms and ourselves was likely so we had to return to the well-trodden path. One of the girls not of the dancing fraternity was amazed when she realised that the jungle, as she called it, was where we trailed just to go to a dance.

"Good Lord you must be keen on dancing," she said, "I wouldn't walk through here at night for anything!"

"Sometimes it's moonlight," said Struggles, "then it's light as day."

"That has happened once," I broke in, ever the one to play things down, "the only thing that worries me is whether I'll tear my stockings or get my eye poked out with a branch."

When we reached the clearing it was empty of vehicles, no one in sight, no sound but the birds. We walked round to the front, everything closed up, not a sign of life anywhere, it seemed impossible that we had danced there only a few nights ago. Because it was wartime it must open only in the evenings we agreed. The drive stretched through more woodland, presumably to a road. We could see the glimmer of water and

walked towards it, planning to sit beside the lake. It was such a
tangle we gave up the idea and sat on some felled trees in a
clearing instead. The sun was warm on our backs and it was
only early April. The smell from the wood, newly cut, was
strong and reminded me of my father's shed; he was a carpenter.
I could identify most woods by their smell. Sitting there eating
our chocolate, we enjoyed the sun, the trees and the brief spell
of freedom. We discussed the past few weeks and speculated on
the next few, tried to make guesses where we would be sent at
the end of our training and what it would sound like when four
big guns were firing close by. All too soon it was time to make
our way back to the barracks and "Goodbye California
Country Club" again, having already said it the last time we
were dancing there. Rissoles again for the evening meal, a cup
of tea in the NAAFI and our departure from the Royal Artillery
Barracks at Arborfield under cover of darkness, to an east-
coast Firing Camp. Troop movements were always made at
night. A month ago girls and men had entered the barracks in
twos and threes, now they were leaving as one complete unit.
We had covered a lot of ground in four short weeks, acquired
skills and learned a little of army life. We had much more to
learn, much more to accomplish before peace was to come to
our land.

Fire Power

Weybourne, Norfolk, cold and windy. A target plane flew over the sea, C Section were firing at the sleeve (target) towed by a plane. It wasn't as haphazard as it sounds for the sky was free from RAF planes at certain times to enable gun teams to practice. An irate pilot radioed down to the Command Post. "Tell them I'm pulling the bloody thing not pushing it." We had been laying on the plane instead of the sleeve.

We suffered hours and hours of Command Post drill, lining up for action and emergency procedure. From all over the camp we sped to the Command Post when the alarm was sounded, again and again and again. Speed was essential and those who didn't move fast soon learned how – all this, wearing full kit. The men were trained this way and so were the ATS. The respirators were a problem for the well-endowed ATS until they learned to hitch them well up under chins. We were timed from the sounding of the alarm to the report "On Target" and were expected to knock seconds off each time. The first time the ATS heard the guns fire it was frightening, but exciting too, actually training with shells which exploded made it real. Even so we had a lot more to learn; it would be vastly different when enemy planes were above us. At Arborfield we had learned to use the instruments; at Weybourne we fetched and carried the heavy batteries needed to power them, learned how to top them up with distilled water and how to connect and disconnect leads. There too we had lectures and marching drill.

Weybourne for me will always conjure up the sight of a lone ATS figure being marched every evening for a week. Up and down and across the parade square backwards and forwards. Wearing full kit, the lot, giving the orders, a male Sergeant. She was a Defaulter; her crime – she had gone absent without leave to spend time with her sailor husband who was on embarkation leave. The army term Defaulter meant "being on a Charge"; sins leading to this state could be failure to carry out an order, being late on parade, losing kit, answering back to a non-commissioned officer (NCO), dumb insolence (which was thinking what you would say if you did answer back!), and being absent without leave (AWOL). Being put on a charge led to being marched by a Sergeant and an escort to the Orderly Room and told to remove your hat. You stood to attention before an officer (ATS if the Defaulter was female), while the Sergeant read out the Charge (crime). The officer then meted out the punishment. That could be from seven to fourteen days Confined to Barracks (CB), sometimes loss of pay and always Fatigues and Extra Duties after ordinary duties, unpleasant ones usually. A Sergeant could put you on extra fatigues without putting you on a charge.

At Weybourne too we were free after evening meal except on Kit Inspection nights. A dance was held each Sunday in camp, which was greatly looked forward to. There weren't any other dances, not that we could find. The nearest place was Holt and consisted of a railway station and a few houses. Further on was Sheringham, quite a long way, but we did walk there sometimes and bought chips.

At that time the threat of Britain being invaded by sea was a possibility and we had been taught the procedure for this emergency. One night we were rudely awakened, a stick was being rattled along the side of our corrugated tin hut, guaranteed to penetrate the dreams of even the soundest of sleepers. This was the signal for Invasion Alarm, the drill for ATS was quickly into battledress carrying respirator and gas cape, Hut Corporals to march sections to waiting lorries, ATS then transported elsewhere. We never found out where elsewhere was, for after crouching for what seemed like hours in cold dark army lorries we were all thankfully sent back to bed. It was no use asking whether it had been a real alarm or just a rehearsal for the real thing, security was always maintained and we'd learned from Security Lectures that it was imperative to say nothing outside camp or in letters about our army life. Indeed there was much wrinkling of brows when writing letters, even the weather was a doubtful subject. The weather at Weybourne was much colder than we'd been experiencing, Spring hadn't arrived. We used to sing a lovely song, the first line was "Spring will be a little late this year." It went on, "A little late arriving in my lonely world over here," a sentimental song of course. Many good songs were written during the war years; we sung our way through them all and loved them.

On our walks through the lanes to Sheringham it was eerie to see, moving slowly and quietly along the hedges and ditches in the fields, soldiers in camouflage dress. The moving figures were not easy to spot, just a movement here and there. The hedges in the area were all low and just two fields lay between the lane and the sea. We tried to count them, there seemed to be hundreds. As we talked about the invasion threat and hoped that it would never happen, the sight of those slowly creeping columns along the hedgerows was comforting. One of our number voiced the thoughts of us all when she remarked, "Well I hope it doesn't happen till we've had a bash anyway."

If the ATS used the NAAFI in the evenings we had to change into Service Dress which was a bind. It meant cleaning buttons for one thing; we had all got used to wearing the comfortable battledress. Thankfully, once we were on an operational site, the rule didn't apply. Before the war hardly any of us had ever worn trousers, it was considered very daring. Women's trousers were called slacks and, although they were fashionable in America and featured in magazines, not many women in Britain were actually seen wearing them. Attitudes to women's clothes changed quickly after war began. Apart from being a comfortable garment to wear while carrying out a variety of tasks, they were necessary when women took over men's jobs. For decorum, for ease of movement and for safety, women wore boilersuits on munitions, working on machinery and on the railway. Trousers were worn in the Fire Service and on numerous other occasions.

NAAFI canteens varied from place to place, both in quality of food and goods for sale. Apart from the aforementioned rationed cigarettes and chocolate, they sold toothpaste and other toiletries; soap too was rationed. Kit-cleaning materials, Blanco Brasso, shoe polish and dubbin, were the main stock in trade however. Boots had to be dubbined, not polished, but some girls liked shiny boots and risked using polish. Sometimes on parade, an Orderly Officer would tell the Orderly Sergeant to rub a finger across a boot. Woe betide that girl if a brown stain appeared. For some reason, a tin of Brasso was the easiest thing in the world to knock over and the ensuing mess was hard to clean off.

A few of us fancied some Ox Blood shoe polish we saw on the NAAFI shelves. As its name implies it was red, we had thought it would be brown with a red tinge, but it was undoubtedly red. Church Parade was every Sunday as at Durham and Arborfield and taken by an Army Padre. The Sunday after we'd bought the polish we paraded and were inspected, the ATS wearing service dress. Every wearer of Ox Blooded shoes was sent off the Parade Ground in disgrace to re-do the offending footwear and to join the service as quickly as possible. It wasn't really our fault, we grumbled, what was it doing on the NAAFI shelves if we were not allowed to use it? One of the unexplained army quirks!

During the morning breaks, the two batteries training used the NAAFI at separate times, there was never enough time to stand in the queue, get served and consume whatever you had purchased. It was in the queue that we did our chattering, relaxing from the tense atmosphere of the Command Post. There was no time to sit down even if you got served. Dreaded was the sound of a whistle and a bellow "C Section outside at the double," when you had either just reached the counter or were just carrying a mug of tea away from it: this happened often.

On the walls were drawings of various characters with derogatory remarks, Hitler of course was one and a little fellow known as Chad. I think that character was invented by one of the newspaper cartoonists and some very clever and funny comments appeared nationwide chalked on walls, bomb sites, all over the place. Chad himself was depicted as half a face with a big nose peeping over a wall, a bald head with five hairs sticking up. The captions were the main feature.

Struggles and I saw less and less of each other at Weybourne, each of us involved more with our own sections. Only one dance a week to look forward to, we talked of the California Club and wondered who our Cadet Bandsmen would be dancing with. At the camp dance the music was home grown, a piano, drums and maybe a wind instrument. There was always someone in the army who could play a piano, male or female, good, bad or indifferent. One night a different colour uniform appeared, two to be exact, RAF Pilots. Blown in from I know not where, they were probably lost! Struggles and I happened to be near the door and I was swept on to the dance floor as quickly as it takes to say "Can I have this dance?" followed by Struggles and the second RAF uniform. My partner was a good dancer, the other was passable, they stayed with us and were good company until nearly the end of the dance when they departed in an old banger of a car. From whence they came we knew not, or where they were going, security prevailed. For Struggles and I the encounter with the two boys who had arrived after the interval brightened up the rest of the evening considerably. They were different somehow, it wasn't just the uniforms, it was their attitude, everything was a joke. We laughed together as Struggles and I hadn't laughed since leaving Arborfield. Hopefully we attended the next camp dance and the next, but we never saw them again.

A tragic accident happened in the other battery one day while we were at Weybourne. Firing Practice was in progress when a shell exploded inside the breach of one of the guns. Bits flew in all directions and the Loading Tray sliced the head off the gunner standing nearest. It was no one's fault, accidents did happen. The incident cast a gloom over us all and underlined the dangers of using weapons.

Our days were filled with firing practice and Command Post drill. We were timed endlessly on the speed it took us to be in action from the moment the alarm was heard to the report "On Target". There were more lectures, more aircraft recognition tests, kit inspections, hut inspections, medical inspections, no idle hours or idle hands. The Devil would have fared badly at Weybourne looking for idle hands.

At last the day dawned when we were a fully trained battery

with its complement of officers. Commanding Officer Major Wheatcroft (CO), two Captains (one for each half of the Battery), four Lieutenants, a Sergeant Major and the correct number of Sergeants and Bombardiers to operate two gunsites plus gunners, male and female. In charge of ATS administration Miss Boardman, Junior Commander, in rank equivalent to Captain and a junior officer for each site. Struggles and I were to be in different halves, the split was now final and the distances between the two sites would make contact between us unlikely, we each now belonged to a set group. While at Firing Camp, ATS in the same operational teams had been housed in the same huts, to this effect each hut represented a kind of household. Girls were responsible for cleaning their own quarters, later on site they would pride themselves on making them as homelike as authority would allow, which wasn't very much in our battery. When the team I was in went to another battery in the regiment for a week to train ATS on new equipment, we envied them the concessions granted. The ATS huts looked like home from home and made ours look pretty bare in comparison.

In three months the ATS had learned new skills, how to work side by side with male gunners as part of a team and to obey orders without question. Each one of us had settled down into a routine and the pattern that our lives would follow from then onwards. Apart from the operational aspect, the girls accepted regimentation resignedly, but were as efficient as the men in everything required of a gunner.

The RA officers must have been relieved as much as anything else to realise that in spite of all their misgivings about the wisdom of mixed batteries, their doubts about the ability of girls, their worst fears had been proved groundless. The girls performance on the Command Post had been equal to any male gunner and so with a few reservations they could go on leave with a lightening of the burden which landed on their shoulders a few months ago.

Everyone was being given a breathing space, a railway warrant and a pass for nine days leave. All except for a small number who would be on the Advance Party; they would proceed to the allocated gunsite near Stockton-on-Tees to take over from the battery already there. The Advance Party would have their leave on the return of the others. Stockton-on-Tees was a busy port and a Bomber Station was in the vicinity. Our job would be to defend these.

Our kitbags were taken to Holt by truck, the Battery marched there in full kit. Everyone boarded the same train *en route* for Norwich from whence we travelled in different directions to the homes we had left years ago, or so it seemed. The kitbags were heavy, how we girls managed to haul them, plus all our other accoutrements on the journey to our homes, I'll never know. Kitbags, when full, resembled a fat sausage. They were fastened by a cord threaded through the top. The soldiers carried them on their shoulders and we tried to do likewise. I found it impossible to carry mine on my shoulders or anywhere else and resorted to dragging it on and off buses and trains. Later on in the war ATS kitbags were designed and issued which had two carrying handles.

The girl gunners had set out from their homes in February and perhaps some of them had felt a little uncertain. They journeyed back in early May full of self assurance and pride. The timid ones less timid and the cocky ones less cocky. We had all grown up a little.

First Leave

At Norwich station, a sea of khaki dispersed and mingled with the other travellers. Trains were not always guaranteed to take the route as advertised and it was foolish to expect every train to run on time. Some of us had much longer journeys to face than others. In C Section one girl was heading for the Isle of Skye, it would take her nearly two days to reach home. Another to Cornwall, one to the far corner of Wales and the rest of us somewhere in between.

On arrival at the station the ATS had divested themselves of the kit hanging round their necks, tied the gas capes to kitbags and slung the respirators, satchel fashion as they were worn when not on duty. Joyfully we set off on our first leave, kitbags just another little inconvenience. As it turned out, mine came in very useful for sitting on in trains and on station platforms. I had to change trains at least twice and in the dim lighting at one station, offended a Naval officer's dignity by mistaking him for a member of the station staff. "No I don't know when the next damn train goes" he snapped. "I'm not a porter." I walked away feeling a bit silly and a WAAF said as I passed her, "I've just asked him about trains, he's a Naval officer, it's a good job we're not Wrens."

Wrens were so called, it being an easy way of saying Women's Royal Naval Service. One of my aunts always called them, "Warens," using the initials as a word. It was ages before my uncle could decipher that fact; she continued to call them Warens just the same. I answered the WAAF, "If we had been WRNS we'd have known that he wasn't a porter." We chatted for a while, both of us knowing better than to ask where the other was stationed with posters all round. Walls have ears and Careless talks costs lives. The slogans posted in public places were taken seriously by those in uniform and if anyone was heard "sounding off", particularly in a boastful manner, he would quickly be told in Army, Navy or Air Force terms what to do! Leave and boyfriends thus were safe subjects, so we discoursed on this matter. The WAAF had been in uniform some months, it was her second leave and she hoped her boyfriend would be at the station to meet her. He was a soldier and would be spending part of his leave with her parents. The two of them were going to buy an engagement ring the WAAF told me proudly, then both of them would stay with the boy's mother for the remainder of the leave. No doubt points would have been saved up for such an occasion as an engagement party. For weddings and christenings, sugar, tins of spam and salmon would be hoarded like gold in households, humble or otherwise. Eventually salmon disappeared from shop shelves.

The WAAF's train arrived and puffed its way out, we waved to each other and my train came soon afterwards. I was to share many such fleeting confidences from men and girls, married and single, over the next few years while travelling to and from leave. On trains sometimes stuck in sidings for ages while a more important cargo steamed through, on station platforms in the middle of the night and in canteens; hopes, dreams, tragedies, heartaches, worries and joys were unfolded by stranger to stranger in those days of enforced separation.

In wartime the trains were always crowded, once on you were jammed. Rarely did I get a seat, corridors would be filled with uniformed bodies and kitbags. When the train stopped at a station, passengers had to climb over it all to get out. The light bulbs in the carriages were low, about the equivalent of one candle power, so it was very gloomy if you were travelling during the hours of darkness. Some played cards, though how they could tell hearts from spades I don't know. The carriages had blinds, but I suppose for the sake of safety the lighting had to be dim.

It was wonderful to be at home sitting round a cosy fire with Mum and my brother. I hadn't seen a fire since leaving home. Sitting there watching the flames with a kettle gently hissing on the hob was all I needed just then. My father was out and my sister too. Though younger than I, it appeared that my sister was being allowed more freedom than I had enjoyed. Mum said Jean had gone to the pictures with two friends, but my brother told me later that she was meeting a soldier. My sister told me that she had to bribe our brother not to tell tales. He had a knack of finding out her plans especially if he was required sometimes to carry messages on her behalf.

The actual fireplace at home that first night was unfamiliar but no less welcoming for all that. While I had been away the family had moved house, not far away, two or three miles up the hill, so it wasn't really strange territory. The village of Ansley was a long winding road with houses of various ages and styles on either side. It started from a crossroads curving away from the main road, which led to the small town of Nuneaton in one direction and the village of Arley in the other. The fourth road led to the village of Galley Common.

At the centre of the so-called crossroads stood a huge oak tree which had a wooden seat fastened round its great girth. Feet made pathways across the grassed circle surrounding it. On fine days old men would gather beneath the oak's branches as no doubt centuries of old men had gathered before. It was a good vantage point, everything was visible on the four roads. Before the war that wouldn't have been much, not on wheels anyway. A bus night and morning to take people to work, cyclists, a few farm carts and maybe an odd tractor. At the other end of the village stood the church, the school and the war memorial to the fallen in the Great War. Steps led up to the memorial; two large guns stood on either side as if guarding the church and school. Ironically, the guns were carted off along with many iron gates and railings, some of them beautiful and of antique value. Britain needed the metal to make more weapons and regretfully householders saw their precious property dismantled and taken away for the War Effort.

A short way along from the crossroads, the first building of any significance to some people was the Lord Nelson Inn. Our cottage was down a lane with several others behind the inn. A shop on the corner of the lane and another further down the road were typical village shops stocking everything from safety pins to paraffin oil as well as groceries. The other hostelry, the

Boot Inn, was at the end of the village and between the inns was the Ansley Working Men's Club – a wooden structure containing a bar, a concert room and a small billiard room where mothers and children sat while the men drank in the bar. A large grassed area with seats and tables where families could sit in summer months was at the back. People would walk across the fields from Arley, Hill Top and Galley Common at weekends, to sit and chat with other mothers. It was mainly women who sat outside with their children, they usually walked back home earlier than husbands to put children to bed.

The first morning of my leave I certainly enjoyed staying in bed as long as I liked. The house was quiet, it felt strange. For three months I had never been alone, now I was, except for the dog. After breakfast I went outside to explore, it had been dark on my arrival. The dog followed me into the garden, a couple of apple trees grew at the side and a rather stunted looking damson tree. A lean-to structure was built on to the garden side of the cottage which appeared to be used for storing coal, garden tools, bicycles and whatever else was deemed might come in useful one day – nothing was ever thrown away. A shed stood at the back of the cottage which on investigation turned out to be my father's workshop, for when I opened the door, the delightful scent of different woods assailed my nostrils. I would have recognised it even if I had been blindfolded. Still wearing my dressing gown I walked into the lane. Playing at being a lady, Mum would have said if she'd been there. It would have been nice if she had been. That first morning I was at home but she, like lots of other mums, was on munitions and after working all day in a factory, would come home to clean and cook for her family.

One end of the lane led to the main road through the village and the other to a stile over which lay a path through the fields. Not a soul was in sight as I looked around at the few scattered cottages; the dog suddenly darted past and ran to the stile barking. He ran back to me still barking, then to the stile again. "All right then," I shouted at him "go!" He streaked underneath the stile and away to the end of the field on some business of his own. I stood leaning over the stile for a time then called to him and we went indoors to get dressed. My wardrobe (hooks behind a curtain) contents did not look exciting, a little jaded perhaps. It was obvious my sister had borrowed some of them, we were the same size except for shoes. It was too much to expect to find a pair of unladdered stockings, I would just have to wear my army ones. Lucky it wasn't exactly summer, but a rather cool May, so a skirt and flat shoes would not look out of place. Wearing pretty undies (untouched it seemed), was a pleasure; to go hatless was a joy when for weeks a hat out of doors, which was most of the time, had been compulsory.

Off I went along the road towards the far end of the village, hoping to meet someone to say hello to, but it was like the town of Hamelin after the Pied Piper had led all the children away and the parents had gone looking for them. Everyone was either at work or in bed after nightshift. Schoolchildren were at school, the elderly, because it was cold, were indoors. There must be someone, I thought, besides me; then I spied coming toward me two girls pushing prams. Of course they knew about me, in a village everyone knows everything, well almost everything, of what is going on. We chatted a while and I discovered that the first thing you are asked when on leave from the Forces is "When are you going back?" That apart, I enjoyed the chat and learned that Astley Castle, a few miles away, had been requisitioned by the army and the soldiers billeted there used the village pubs and the "Club". The Army Medical Corps were in residence at the castle which was being used as a surgery, not a hospital. Only a small number of personnel were stationed there, mainly ambulance drivers. The two young mums mourned the fact that for them, any thoughts of enjoying a drink with the Medical Corps would be strictly taboo. So would any dances likely to be held in the club? Their husbands were away in the Forces and the wives of any servicemen would be watched diligently by parents and in-laws to make sure they didn't stray from the straight and narrow. It was much easier in a village, especially such a small one as this, though there did occur a small scandal or two. Looking at the well-wrapped bundles in the prams with only their chubby faces showing, I didn't think the two of them really meant the regret they voiced about not being free to go malarking as they called it. We went our separate ways, I towards the school when I remembered that Sandy my brother would not be coming out of school till 4 p.m., so I turned back at the end of the houses.

This wasn't quite as I'd expected, I don't really know what I had expected to be honest. I hadn't thought any further than the actual arriving home. As I neared the Lord Nelson Inn, I could see the owner of the shop outside cleaning the shop windows. "Hell" she called "you must be Vera the other one, I knew you were coming on leave, when are you going back?" She didn't wait for an answer but went on, "A bit quieter than the army eh? They're all in bed, at work, or at school except the ones playing truant that is and they'll be out of sight somewhere in the woods or fields till the others come out of school." I stood watching her rubbing away at the window, she stepped down from the stool she was standing on, looked along the road and said "There'll be a slight flutter of life at about midday when the pubs open, the old 'uns will appear from doors within a minute or two of each other as if by magic, and like a steady stream of ants they will file to their own drinking holes; come inside it's parky out here."

I followed her into the shop, there was still not a soul about. Village shops at one time used to be the hub of village life where all the gossip was exchanged, advice given, asked or unasked, and to sit there on a bag of potatoes looking through the glass in the shop door at a still landscape seemed unnatural. Alice, for that was her name, was a spinster with a wry sense of humour. I heard quite a lot about village doings during the hour spent with her, none of which meant very much to me, not knowing at that time who was who.

Carefully, she cut a cigarette in half and offered me one half. I told her I didn't smoke which surprised her. She put the proffered half on an empty shelf and said, "Your sister does. I've heard you're the quiet one though and they are usually the ones to watch." It was meant as a joke but she gave me a sly grin as she said it. It appeared that considering the age gap between my sister and Alice they were the best of friends and shared many a cigarette and confidences. Another thing I learned, Alice was very broadminded, nothing could shock her and she asked a great many questions which was how she acquired her knowledge of all that went on. She got nothing out of me regarding my military career naturally, just that yes I was enjoying it, was glad to be home, no I hadn't got a regular chap.

"You might get one now," she said, "there are some soldiers at the castle, they come into the village, there's another lot at Hill Top billeted in the Mission Hut but they use The Fir Tree at Arley." I thought to myself, if I was seen talking to a soldier, would Alice be asking me the next time I saw her whether I was "going out" with him? "It's twelve o'clock, if you look out, you'll see them, poor old souls." That from her who looked as old as the hills herself, I found amusing. I got up, said it had been nice talking to her and went out. She called after me to be good and if I couldn't be good to be careful.

In the afternoon I rushed to the corner to catch the bus into Nuneaton, only three buses a day passed the crossroads. People working in Coventry on munitions travelled in special buses supplied by the factories. They only picked up and dropped passengers at the crossroads, meaning a long walk for Ansley dwellers, especially those at the far end. In town I didn't meet anyone I knew. It was the same everywhere, people at work, only the elderly and mothers with children under school age and babies were about in the streets. I couldn't use the Forces canteen not being in uniform. There were a few uniforms about, on leave I supposed, and wondered if they felt as out of place as I did. Oh no, it wasn't as wonderful, this leave, as I'd expected it to be. I couldn't go back home, there wasn't a bus till much later to take people home from work, so I passed the time looking in shops at things I couldn't afford till it was time to catch the bus. At the bus stop I met quite a number of girls I knew, things started to get better. I arranged to go dancing one night in town, there was church concert at The Drum, that much loved place. That was a start, at the crossroads I stepped off the bus lighter in spirit and waved to my friends who lived in Arley.

Earlier I had left an empty house, on my return it was normal again, busy, everyone in from work and school, a smell of cooking, dishes rattling – home, as I remembered it. Mum told me that her friend further up the lane had asked her to take me to the Nelson for a drink that evening so I would be seeing the inside for the first time. Although I had sampled alcohol at the California Country Club, never before had I gone inside a pub at home. I had been in the Social Club with Mum an odd time, but that really didn't count as sometimes there were as many children as adults in there. I decided after another look behind my curtain to don my uniform for the evening. There was nothing suitable or glamorous enough for my debut at the pub. Jean wasn't joining us, she had other fish to fry it seemed. Glibly words could roll off her tongue with a ring of truth that satisfied the parents. If my brother winked at me I guessed that what she had imparted did only have a very faint ring of truth. The three years between my sister and I might well have been ten years. We were not a bit alike except in looks, in fact when we were small, people would take us for twins. She never told me any secrets nor did I tell her any of mine. When we were younger we played with the same children all together, but as we grew older we each had our own set of friends. A little while after my first leave, Jean followed me into khaki, under age. I don't quite know how she managed it but she did. My parents could have gone after her and insisted on her release but they didn't. She was attached after her training to the Royal Electrical Mechanical Engineers (REME).

With buttons and shoes shined to perfection, Mum and I set off up the lane. Dad would be in the bar, but we made our way into the big room, so called because it was where they held suppers or receptions. A bare wooden floor and wooden seats, there wasn't much comfort in village pubs then, only the liquid imbibed therein. Someone waved to us from a corner table and we went over to join Mum's friend and three ladies of similar age. Everyone knew who I was of course, only one other girl besides myself was in the Forces from the village and she was in the WAAF. We never met in all the war years oddly enough, not until we were demobbed. I learned all about her in due course from Alice at the shop, her name was Amelia Bennet. I've no doubt that she heard of my doings from the same source and when we did eventually meet, it wasn't as strangers, for I had already met her brother on a leave, he also wore air-force blue. It was going to be all female that night it appeared, the husbands were all in the bar. Only the henpecked ones sit with their wives, I was told; they talk their men's talk and we talk about them, laughter all round. Mum's friend brought our drinks, I thought mine was orange juice till I tasted it. I must have made a face, she said, "Get it down you, it will do you good; it's a ladies' drink, gin and orange." I tried another sip and decided I liked it. They all, with the exception of my Mum, thought that because I was in the army I was an experienced drinker and were surprised to find I wasn't. In fact up to then, the sum total of my experience was, beer which I didn't like, cider ditto, guinness and shandy I could tolerate, brandy which I'd choked over and babycham.

The evening passed pleasantly enough, they were a jolly bunch recounting stories of food queues in town, the foreman at the factories, what men's shirt tails could be turned into by an ingenious needlewoman and what the husband of one of them had said when he discovered all his shirts cut at waist level. Grumbles there were about the upset of war, as one called it. I suppose that was as good a word as any, but rather milder than some I'd heard.

As I snuggled down in bed after my first full day of leave, I was in a happier frame of mind. Maybe the gin had a little to do with that, but there was the concert to look forward to and the dance at the Co-op Hall in town. Who knew what else there might be? I had been a little naive to expect everything would be just the same as when I had left three months ago. The crowd I'd gone to dances with, known since schooldays, were doing other things. Courting steady, one or two even planning weddings. Not the sort of weddings we had discussed before the war where we had vied with each other in describing the dresses we would wear as we swept down the aisle in clouds of tulle and lace. All would not be wearing long white gowns unless borrowed, the wedding feast would not be lavish and it would be highly unlikely if a honeymoon away was possible. Some weddings would be a little premature. The pattern used to be, girl met boy, street corner chats and at dances boy and girl only danced with each other. Walk home after dance, though in a crowd walk together. Walks through fields and woods although meeting at road end or even right outside the village. Then nervously the girl asked mother if boy could come to Sunday tea, mother would inform father and whether permission was given or not would depend on what parents knew about boy. Of course up to then it wouldn't have been openly discussed, a well known secret in fact. Boy came to

Sunday tea, then the whole village understood that with parental approval, boy and girl were courting. In turn, girl would be invited to boy's home and they would each be warned separately of the dire consequences of "getting into trouble". Everyone would start to save up, boy for an engagement ring, girl for her "bottom drawer", girl's parents for the wedding. Only the boy's parents could sit back unless they had a daughter in the same situation. A few couples didn't reach the engagement stage for one reason or another and the girl's bottom draw would be fairly well equipped before the next liaison began. In those days very few girls' ambitions went beyond a home of their own and children. Most of the relationships continued, however, and quite a number of childhood sweethearts married, though obeying the ritual of Sunday tea. By the end of the "upset" of war, as the lady in the Nelson put it, things had changed.

The bright sunshine awoke me next morning, I knew what I was going to do straight after breakfast. Bicycle hauled out from the shed, tyres pumped hard, and away I went into the lanes, down the long hills; with hair streaming I whizzed along. Not much traffic in the criss-cross of lanes little more than cart tracks, leading only from main ones round to a farm, a cottage or two and back again. Dismounting at the steeper hills, standing at the top to drink in the sight of fields, trees and well-known landmarks, I realised how much I had missed it all.

Uniform again for the evening outing even though it meant cleaning brass, I needed stout shoes for the long walk there and back anyway. The concert turned out to be a play which I enjoyed, more so because I knew some of the amateur cast and it was a comedy. Among the village audience was a lone soldier, he didn't appear to know anyone so he couldn't be on leave I deduced. At the interval when the welcome cup of tea was served, he spoke to me. We were the only two in uniform and on our own. He told me he'd met a girl from the village and they were supposed to be meeting at the door. He had waited till after the performance had begun and then crept in and sat at the back. If she hadn't turned up before the second half began he said mournfully, she won't be coming.

When the play was over, after chatting to people I knew about the actors and other village happenings, I drifted out still chatting. It wasn't the era of a car to every house and most people were using shanks's pony. No one it seemed was going my way or so I thought till I spied a standing figure in the gloom. The soldier had waited for me, he was one of the troop billeted in the Hill Top Mission so I had company nearly all the way. The poor young man was smitten with the missing damsel and went on at great length about her. When he asked me to go to the cinema with him the next evening, I politely declined making some excuse. I certainly did not intend being second best.

After my refusal, polite though it was, I expected to be walking from the Mission alone, but he insisted on accompanying me the rest of the way. I left him at the lane end, thanked him sweetly and said I hoped he would make contact with his dream girl. I didn't want him to know which was my house in case he came knocking on the door. As I passed Alice's closed shop, I thought to myself she's wrong about me being sure to get a chap while I'm on leave if tonight is anything to go by. Anyway I didn't want a chap yet, not in the way she meant, a regular one.

The sun didn't wake me the next day, it was dark, dismal and wet. This was a town day I decided, in uniform, then I could spend a little time in a Forces canteen. One thing I certainly was not going to wear was the groundsheet, my greatcoat would suffice, it withstood quite a lot of rain before getting soaked.

The canteen was warm, I shed my greatcoat and went to the counter. Bless all those ladies who during the war manned the urn and the teapots the length an breadth of the British Isles, in church halls and the like. Cheerful and chatty usually, most had sons, daughters, grandsons and granddaughters away in uniform and hoped that wherever they may be, they might find a canteen staffed by kind mothers and grandmothers too.

After a reasonable time spent in the canteen which was nearly empty (it was busier in the evenings I was told), I went out into the dismal weather and drifted round Woolworths, Marks and Spencer's, the Co-op Stores and the largest store which had a restaurant, Smiths on the Bridge. That was it's name, part of it actually bridges the river running through the town. I was heading towards this and passed two girls standing in a shop doorway, they sniggered and one said loudly "OGS". "What's that?" asked the other. "Don't you know?" answered the first, "it means officer's groundsheet" and they laughed. I was furious, I kept on walking with my head held high, how dare they. I had already learned that ignoring rude comments and pretending not to hear them was the best way of dealing with verbal abuse. There was no doubt about hearing her for she said it loud enough for those on the other side of the street to hear. That was the first time I had heard the slur, but it wasn't the last. I heard it a number of times while serving King and Country and however many times I heard it, the hurt didn't lessen.

After a special workers' lunch at Smiths on the Bridge, I bought stockings with coupons Mum had given me, which saved me from going to the dance with mended stockings, khaki ones or painting my legs (and I was never any good at that). There was a knack in getting the stuff on without patches and I never learned the knack. If you didn't keep shaking the bottle, the colouring agent settled in the bottom.

On the homeward bus a lady sat down beside me. "Hello, I heard you were in the ATS, I suppose you're on leave, when are you going back?" She laughed, "Everyone says that don't they? But tell me because I want you to come to tea before you go back, I want to hear all about what you've been doing." She went on to tell me news of the Arley crowd, one was in the WRNS, two in the WAAF, three in the Land Army and one in the ATS (two counting me). All the ones she mentioned I had been at school with, including her son who was in the RAF. She had a younger son who was still at school and she would so have loved a daughter. Some years later she did get her husband talked round into adopting a two year old girl. Mrs. L. was a kindly person, the sort people took their troubles to, she would give a helping hand to anyone and liked young people round her, so it was with pleasure that I accepted her invitation to tea on Sunday hoping Mum wouldn't mind my not being there at the Sunday tea table. I would only have one Sunday on leave but even with the food shortages it was still special and different to all the other days of the week.

It had hardly stopped raining all day, I looked forward to spending an evening in front of a cheerful fire and hoped the next day would bring sunshine or at least that it would be dry. I planned on doing a few more cycling miles to store up pictures of rivers and streams, woods and hills dressed in their May greenery. To photograph in my memory and hold forth bad days ahead; bad days there had been already and no doubt there would be others. It was a comforting thought that it would all be there when and if I returned.

The next morning was dull but dry, I took the dog for a walk, an unusual treat for him on weekdays, he was let out for a wander first thing and the last one to leave the house in the morning would call him in. The first one in at teatime would let him out again and he would be taken for a run in the evening. He must have thought it was the weekend again, my brother took him for long walks then: not in the direction I intended to go it was apparent. After a pull on the lead and a questioning look from Blackie, I facing one way and he the other, I gave in and went his way. Down towards the stile he went, walking to heel. He stopped at the stile, I dropped the lead for him to go underneath but he stood still and looked at me. "You daft dog," I said. "I thought you wanted to go this way." He gave a short sharp bark. "Oh sorry," I said and unclipped his lead. He ran along the hedge rooting here and there as dogs do and looking round to see if I was following. I don't think he was too sure of my intelligence. We walked through the meadows, which is what we called the fields between our stile and the one leading out to a lane on the way to Galley Common – a mining village built partly in a valley and partly on a hill on which stood the church and the church hall. With fond memories of village dances, I was hoping to see a notice about a dance being held that week but I was unlucky, other notices about other things there were in profusion. I turned away dejected but not for long; the day was mine to do what I liked with, I had someone to talk to (dogs do talk if you bother to listen), and I was treading the paths I'd daydreamed about. We headed up the lane beside the school and on to The Rookery which, apart from a farm and a few cottages, led only to woods and fields. A path wound its way through these and so did we to Ansley Village and home.

After lunch, a watery looking sun came out and so did the cycle. It would have to be a shorter route so to the castle I headed. Astley couldn't be called a village by any stretch of the imagination, it was a hamlet. A church, a castle, a short row of cottages outside the church gates and two farms were the sum total of its buildings – a quiet backwater and one of my favourite places. Propping my cycle against the wall outside the gate, I entered the churchyard and went to the kissing gate at the far end. The gate opened on to a lane leading past the castle, but the best view of the castle outline was from the kissing gate, the moat and outer wall curving round near the churchyard. When I was younger I used to make stories up about the little door which could be seen from the kissing gate. At the foot of the wall a rough path ran round the castle between it and the moat. I used to wonder if anyone had escaped from the castle through the door, if secret trysts had been kept there, all kinds of ifs. Looking then at the neglected moat and the thicket bordering it, I thought it could be the tangled forest in The Sleeping Beauty. A voice from behind startled me, I hadn't heard a footstep.

"Not thinking of doing away with yourself are you?" the voice said. I turned round, "Not going to jump in are you?" it went on.

"You made me jump, I don't think it would be easy to drown in that overgrown water; it's a shame it's got like that," I retorted.

"Well we aren't the Pioneer Corps," the young man said "we're the RAMC." There was only a small contingent billeted in part of the castle. He told me most of the rooms were locked as furniture and pictures were still there. He invited me in to look around. I hesitated, much as I desired to be inside that castle, I didn't want to sneak in like a thief. Seeing my reluctance the soldier said he'd ask Sarge, surgery was over, Medical Officer gone, only a few ambulance drivers were about anyway. I said I'd love to see inside the castle, but would only go in if his Sergeant said I could. I waited, then from the little door I saw him waving, I lost no time in running through the gate, over the bridge, through the gap in the wall and down the steep path to the little door. It opened into a small courtyard outside the kitchen quarter.

I followed him through the kitchen as he was saying "Here she is then and Sarge says its time for a brew up and we'll all have some of your seed cake."

"Ho do," to me and "Rightho Jack, it'll be ready in a minute, I'll give you a shout," said the cook. I followed Jack into a hall, a wide staircase swept upwards, portraits hung on the panelled walls.

"In here," he said, going through a door into a large airy room, "We eat in here."

"Aren't you lucky?" I sighed. Huge windows almost to the floor looked out on to a large courtyard which had a maze in the centre, though so overgrown it was difficult to recognise it was a maze. What a shame I thought, just like the moat. The high wall at the far side of the courtyard had narrow openings like windows through which Astley Pool could be seen. The moat was below the wall I found when I walked out to see the overgrown garden.

A shout came from the kitchen and Jack went to fetch the tea and seed cake which turned out to be delicious. A pity we weren't eating from china plates and drinking tea from delicate cups, I thought. I never saw the Sergeant, Jack said he never bothered them if they didn't bother him. Not at all like the Royal Artillery I told him. As I was leaving, the cook asked me if I would like to see the kittens, they were adorable as all baby creatures are. The mother cat was a tabby, three kittens were the same and one was black with white paws. The cook said he would have to find homes for them soon and gave me an enquiring look. Jack took me and the cycle as far as the crossroads in one of the ambulances although I told him that a drop of rain wouldn't hurt me. He said he had to take the vehicle somewhere in that direction anyway and would I meet him in the Social Club that evening?

I was torn between wearing "civvies" with my new stockings, risking a ladder or showing how smart I could be in uniform with the RA insignia shining and wearing the white gunner's lanyard. In the end the worry about stockings for the dance settled it, so out came the brasso and the button stick again. This was a flat brass plate with a slot down the centre, buttons slid through the slot enabling them to be polished without marking the cloth. I spent the evening in the club with four of the RAMC, surprisingly they didn't know about ATS on gunsites. I had thought because they were in the army, they would know everything about the other branches. What is more it didn't impress them either, to them the ATS were ATS. Pride goeth before a fall, perhaps not a fall, but my ego was deflated a little and what a waste of Brasso! We all walked out of the club together, they had come in a truck and wanted to give me a lift. My house was only a stone's throw down the road I told them, I didn't want to be seen climbing into an army truck with four soldiers, Jack said he would walk with me and the others would wait at the corner for him. We said our Goodnight beside Alice's dark closed shop and made a date for the next afternoon to go to the Palace cinema in Nuneaton. I couldn't meet him in the evening I told him, for I was meeting girlfriends to go dancing. He wasn't a dancer I had already discovered, which was a pity: still, my leave was not turning out too badly I thought.

I enjoyed the film, the Pathe Gazette Newsreel and Jack's company, he was slightly amorous in the darkened cinema. We had tea in a cafe then went home, I to make ready for the dance and he to join his mates. He had arranged with one of them to pick us up in Nuneaton in an army vehicle! Hooray the RAMC!

A better bus service operated on Saturdays. I still had to leave before the dance ended, but so had all the rest who lived out of town unless they walked home. I had a wonderful evening, the Co-op Hall had a beautiful floor, the band was excellent and the time passed all too quickly.

My leave passed quickly too, I went to tea at Astley Castle again by invitation from the cook, for something better than seed cake he told me – one of his special cakes. Supper and gossip one evening with a group of schoolfriends, another date with Jack at The Palace cinema. Alice and I had a last session sitting on the sack of potatoes, I told her how wrong her prophecy had been. Jack had told me on our last date that he was courting a girl back home.

"It's a good job you didn't fall in love with him then," she laughed.

"How do you know I didn't?"

"Because you haven't got stars in your eyes," was her reply.

You're In the Army Now

The trains going north were just as crowded as the day I'd set out for home. Changing trains, hauling kitbag from platform to platform, up steps, down steps and arriving in Stockton-on-Tees too late to reach the camp on time was frustrating. If (the little word that matters much) the trains had run as scheduled, I should have had plenty of time to get a bus to the end of the road and drag myself plus kit into the Guardroom to report.

I hadn't seen any of my fellow gunners on the journey, but some must have been on the same train for when the crowd spilled out on the platform amid a welter of arms, legs, respirators, steel helmets, gas capes and kitbags, familiar faces emerged from the mass of khaki. I wasn't the only one going to be late it seemed. Late was not the term used by the Guard Commander, AWOL we were, from the minute we should have signed in. All of us were put on a charge immediately: not a good start. My spirits were at their lowest ebb.

It was pointed out that it was our responsibility to report on time, regardless of transport problems. It took me a long time to get over the disgrace of being a Defaulter on my very first day on a gunsite. We received seven days CB and a stern lecture. Some weeks later we did manage to laugh about it, but for a time we felt like lepers and not one of us ever forgot the incident or the cutting remark made by a Sergeant, "You're in the army now and don't you ever forget it." He for one was determined that we would never be allowed to. The sites were known by letter – we were F for Freddy, the other half of the battery was

G for George and sited at Hartlepool. F site was at Hartburn, a few miles from Stockton-on-Tees along the Darlington road. Hartburn was only a string of houses on one side of a road and fields on the other. A little way past the houses was the gunsite, mainly Nissen huts and of course the guns. There were twelve of us in hut 10, Gunners Atterton, Amy, Crisp, Hague, Hunt, McInnes, Odgers, Stevenson, Thomson, Urquhart, Wellsbury and another whose name I can't recall as she was with us for only a short time. A few nicknames did evolve as time passed. The beds, thankfully, were not bunk beds, a shelf ran above them the length of the hut, twelve wooden boxes for ATS kit. May had, thankfully, warmed up and one of the most vivid memories I have of F site is sitting on the steps of the hut counting the bombers from a nearby airfield. As they swept over our heads, heavily laden on their way to Germany in the dusk, we knew full well that they wouldn't all be coming back.

Air raids were mainly at night for us too. When the alarm sounded it was for real, this was it and we were part of it all. The first time the loud bell shrilled, C section was on manning duty. A bell was installed in every hut on site, and outside the dining hall hung a large triangle of metal and a gong. Whoever was nearest to this and not on one of the manning teams would bang on it till everyone on site was deafened. We tumbled out of beds into battledress on top of pyjamas, boots unlaced, fastening respirators as we ran, steel helmets bouncing if the wearer hadn't adjusted the strap properly. This we had practised many times, but never in the dark. Swiftly and silently each girl ran to her post and carried out what she had been trained to do. Fear was absent, everyone was too busy carrying out their own task to be conscious of fear. Down in the huts there was fear, not many admitted to this, however. If they did it was to say they worried whether the ones in the Command Post would do their job properly. During air raids we would all rather be on the Command Post than anywhere else. If you weren't, there was nothing to do but sit in the hut wearing steel helmets, hoping that nothing would come down on top of it.

Our guns sounded louder than the ones at Firing Camp, they weren't of course, but this was real action against a real enemy above and with all the other guns blasting away in the area the atmosphere was heightened somewhat. Searchlights played their part round about us, they too would be manned by ATS. Beams of light crisscrossed the sky, it was really nothing like Firing Camp at all. Our training had all paid off though, each girl knew exactly what to do and did it. On the order "Stand Down", instruments were switched off, covers put on and everyone dispersed to try and sleep for what was left of the night. Reveille would be the usual time in the morning, however little sleep anyone managed to get.

Once inside the hut, tongues were loosened, all of us chattering at once. The two girls who had not been in a team were sitting on their beds. One of them said to the other, "Go on, tell them then and get it over with."

"Wait till they've all come back from the toilet," the second girl laughed, "I don't want anyone to miss this." When the whole hut was making ready for bed and we were all looking expectantly at the one who had something of interest to impart, the first girl said "It's not funny."

"It is, it is!" chortled the tale teller.

"Well get on with it then," we chorused, "we want some sleep." The guns had been making their din, each blast shaking the ground and rattling the tin roof – the teller went on – she had gone to the toilet and came back to find Hunt sitting white-faced on the edge of her bed clutching her knees with both hands.

"I've been hit in the spine by shrapnel," she said.

The teller continued – "I knew by her face she wasn't joking and looking up at the roof I said, 'There isn't a hole, you can't have been hit, it's your vivid imagination that's all.' Hunt insisted that she had felt a sharp object hit her and would I please look." By this time the victim was in bed with only the top of her head visible and her face to the wall. "When I looked I saw the green glass clock of hers on the bed, it must have edged forward with each gun blast till it toppled off the shelf and hit her."

"Good job it didn't fall on her head, there would have been some blood all right then," laughed the unsympathetic one. There probably would, the clock was heavy, square with sharp corners and had been part of a dressing-table set popular in the thirties. Needless to say the incident caused us much merriment, the more so for it released a little of the tension felt from our first brush with the enemy.

The poor girl didn't live it down for ages and she never quite forgave us for our lack of sympathy. It was only when we were in the same situation during a raid, sitting there listening to the guns and wishing that we were up on the Command Post, that we really understood how Hunt's imagination could have run riot. Shrapnel had been known to pierce tin roofs and our only protection was our steel helmets, no cellars or air raid shelters. We eyed the fire buckets dubiously, one filled with sand and one with water, and breathed a prayer of thankfulness when the guns stopped firing, for the time being.

The site worked on a 24-hr timetable from 2 p.m. till 2 p.m. The main parade at 2 p.m. was the changeover and 24-hr leaves commenced then. Personnel starting leave paraded, were duly inspected and then dismissed. Manning teams were marched to the Command Post to carry out gun drill, sometimes Air Co-operation with the RAF. Sections did manning duty alternate 24 hours. The section not manning were otherwise occupied on Guard Duty at the main gate, Fire Piquet, cookhouse fatigue and general duties which included cleaning ablutions. Prowler Guard was also part of that section's duties.

In theory we were allowed 24 hours' leave every twelve days and evening leave every eight, but it seldom worked out like that. You couldn't plan more than two days ahead, for until you read Battery Orders posted up each morning, no one but the Sergeant responsible for doing the roster knew who would be on it. Friends were not always off duty at the same time; to be fair though, most of the time they were unless swords had been crossed with an NCO.

After the 2 p.m. parade the Guard Commander marched her guard of three sentries to the front of the Guardroom and using the correct RA drill, the Changing of the Guard took place. ATS stood sentry on the main gate from then until 8 p.m. then again at 8 a.m. until the changeover at 2 p.m. Prowler Guard meant walking the perimeter of the site, checking all guns and instruments through the hours of darkness. At the time the possibility of German paratroopers being dropped to attack or sabotage gunsites and airfields was considered. The ATS did all the Prowler Guard duties on F site armed only with a pickaxe handle and a whistle. We did two-hour shifts in pairs. The whistle for emergency, we hoped, would be heard by the sentry on the main gate; the men were armed with rifles and there were four of them. Understandably, we were a little uneasy when on this duty, especially as one of the pair had to go and wake the ones taking over the next shift. Any apprehension felt was not voiced in the hearing of males, always mindful of the phrase "You're in the army now!"

We joked of how we would cope if ever the fears about parachutists became a reality, though secretly some of us were proud of doing Prowler Guard. No one felt like joking, however, when actually walking round a sleeping site, listening to tarpaulin covers on the Command Post and guns flapping in the wind. The two hours seemed endless. Sometimes we'd go down to the dug-out underneath to chat to the two telephonists on duty; not that we were always welcomed though, it would depend who was on duty. Sometimes we'd be told to get prowling and look for invaders, that they felt safer with us up on top, keeping watch. Telephonists were exempt from all guard, their duty hours differed from those of the Fire Controlling Instrument teams. No one had told us about Prowler Guard at training camp. We were to discover as time went by that quite a number of facts about our future life as gunners had not been disclosed at training camp. Whatever work was done on the gunsite, the ATS did their share.

All kinds of vehicles and personnel came to F site, the sentry's duty was to check all identification before raising the barrier. Quite a number of visitors were Despatch Riders (DRs) bringing documents and papers from Regimental Headquarters, which was along the Darlington road. One dark and stormy day with high winds and rain lashing down in sheets, I was standing on sentry duty wearing the elegant rubber groundsheet when up roared a DR on his motorcycle. Assuming him to be one of the regulars, I waved him through without making him delve for his ID. With a beaming smile and a salute, he rode past me. He turned out to be a Security Officer checking on standards. Needless to say I was in trouble with a capital T. Apart from being put on a charge for failing in my duty, I was so angry with myself for letting the ATS down. It took a very long time to control the tears that welled each time the others pulled my leg about it, and they did often. No one escaped being ragged, you eventually learned to accept it with good grace and think of a witty reply if you could.

Other duties included cleaning offices, the NAAFI, the dining hall, lecture rooms, windows, picking up cigarette ends (there shouldn't have been any), washing up, peeling potatoes and preparing vegetables. This was done beneath a shaky tin roof outside the cookhouse, which was supposed to keep the rain out, and it was a cold job. No one liked doing these chores but as there was a group working together, we enjoyed the collective grumbling.

Fire Piquet meant four of you checking every item of fire-fighting equipment on the site. This consisted of a bucket of sand, a bucket of water and a stirrup pump in each hut, including dining hall, lecture room, NAAFI and offices. While testing the pumps we found it a good idea to clean the windows at the same time, unofficially. Sleeping quarters were cleaned in your own time, reveille was at 6.45 a.m., breakfast parade was 7.30 a.m., carrying enamel mug and cutlery: after breakfast, hut inspection by the Orderly Officer accompanied by an NCO. At attention we stood beside our beds, blankets folded in a neat pile, steel helmet on top of the pile. The officer would walk round each bed with eagle eye. If one blanket was slightly uneven the pile would be pulled apart and the owner of it had to fold the pile again.

One particular RA officer was in the habit of doing spot checks accompanied by his Orderly Sergeant while the ATS huts were unoccupied. The officer would run his finger along shelves and window ledges. If dust were found, the occupants of the hut received a scathing lecture and were ordered to clean the hut after duties that evening, and not until it had been inspected by an Orderly NCO could anyone with an evening pass leave the site. We used to wonder what his wife was like. Despite his mania, most of us liked him; in civilian life he taught maths at a Grammar school in Lancashire, so wasn't a regular

soldier. He was in charge of the various lectures we sat through
– manning teams, when not on the guns and Command Post,
were still on training in the lecture hut. Male and female
gunners were kept informed of the current war situation by the
army Bureau of Current Affairs ABCA, (as much as we were
allowed to know of it, that is). Also instigated by the officer
were discussion groups on various subjects, such as what
would Britain be like after the war if we lost the struggle. None
of the ATS had any doubts that we would win; with the women
of Britain fighting – us in particular – we couldn't fail, we told
him. This caused a few derogatory remarks and laughter from
the men, but the officer called for order and the serious
discussion went on. Sometimes we'd have debates, which was
good for the quiet ones who were encouraged to take part. If
encouragement didn't work, it was made an order at the next
session. I enjoyed these debates and learned a lot; not everyone
was enthusiastic. It was one thing, they said, to sit round in the
hut with their own crowd and quite another to speak to a
roomful of people, worse than being at school. Better than
doing fatigues anyway, I thought.

Men and girls were dressed identically on the gun park – steel
helmets, battledress, boots, gaiters and respirators in satchels – it
was a pity the girls didn't wear the same uniform as the men for
fatigues. The men had khaki denim battletop and trousers, we had
khaki denim, but it was a stupid garment. A type of boiler suit
always too short in the arms and legs, shapeless and impractical,
as when using the lavatory it meant partially undressing each time.
We joked about it, naturally; as with all army trials and
tribulations, they were bearable if laughed at. Like convicts we
marched off to cookhouse or wherever our duties lay and
muttered to each other intoning with each step things like

> "*Stalag 10 quick peel*
> *hands in water cold feel*
> *Stalag 10 quick peel*
> *hands in water cold feel*"
> or
> "*Scrape the tins into the swill*
> *Pigs their bellies soon will fill*" and so on.

Another unbecoming part of ATS uniform was PT kit: it consisted of a dark-brown divided skirt of material which creased easily and never looked smart, skimpy so it never looked like a skirt. An orange short-sleeved top with a V-neck (sleeves and neck bound with dark brown) and black plimsolls completed the ensemble. PT was every day outside, sometimes before breakfast. Men and girls had separate sessions for this. PT was another army essential not favoured by all, many were the excuses put forward to avoid the exercise. Unless at their last gasp, not many were excused from this daily ritual, everyone had to be at the peak of fitness, mentally and physically.

Food was sometimes boring, but adequate. Some men liked to sit with the girls, purely mercenary on their part. Some girls were a little faddy about food, others were small eaters and the men thankfully proffered plates to these. Food which would otherwise end up in the pig bin to be collected by a local farmer would be transferred to the hungry. Porridge in winter was a good filler, bread of course, but the margarine ration was small, egg or bacon (not both) and fried bread. Tea was served at all meals from steel buckets. I think sometimes the dining hall (hut) maybe resembled a farmyard, our liquid from a bucket, metal containers held the food whether it was stew or custard. The plates were so heavy you needed two hands to carry one: they would withstand being dropped a number of times without breaking while being washed or dried by the cookhouse fatigue.

Dinner was midday, again we paraded and were marched to the dining hall. All hours until off duty, movement about the site was by marching. Dinner was a two-course meal, sometimes the meat content would be unidentifiable but eatable, though some with finer palates would question that statement. Not a great deal from our plates ended up in the pigswill, however. Puddings were rice, semolina, tapioca, macaroni (the last three I didn't eat, but someone else did), spotted dick, jam roll and a pretence for a sponge pudding with a scrape of jam. This pudding took its name from whatever kind of jam was dolloped on the top of it. Tasteless and colourless, served with watery custard, we didn't call it what the cooks did! Nevertheless, it was consumed by the hungry, even though we didn't all manage to get a taste of jam. Tea, the last meal of the day, was usually something hot like beans on toast, sardines on toast, corned beef fritters or my favourite, cheese dreams. This was cheese sandwiches dipped in batter and fried. Sometimes though it could be just bread, cheese, jam and slab cake.

One day we had a visit from the Stockton-on-Tees Fire Brigade who taught us about fire drill and how to rescue someone from a smoke-filled room. We were taught the "fireman's lift", then in groups we practised what had been demonstrated. For the smoke-filled room, an empty hut was used and every one of us had to try the fireman's lift, first without the smoke and then with the room full of smoke. Used correctly it was surprising how even a 7-stone girl could get another to safety. Again, the ATS were on their mettle aiming to prove that girls were as able as men.

Another day we entered a mustard-gas-filled hut wearing respirators in haversacks on the chest as worn on the Command Post. This was to see how quickly we could get them on our faces at the command. The same day blister gas was sprayed on our hands, this had to be removed with cream and cotton wool (which was always carried in the respirator haversack) as quickly as possible before the skin blistered. The soiled cotton swabs were then buried in a deep hole.

Quite a lot of digging went on while we were on Freddy site. When we took over, the gun emplacements weren't completed nor were there any paths on what had previously been a field. The men concreted the gun pits and the girls made the paths and roadways. All of us had to be instructed how to wield picks, shovels and heavy long-handled hammers. I don't think many of us had ever wheeled a barrow before, half of us certainly could not push one when it was filled with stones. We learned not to fill them more than half full. A load of huge rock-like stones arrived on the site one day and thus began our weeks of hard labour. The ATS were convinced that the concreting job was easier than the road-making. This prison job, as we called it, was done on the 24-hr system too. The section not manning worked on road-making as well as all other duties. Male Sergeants acted as foremen. I remember one shouting at an ATS who was lightly tapping at a lump of rock, "Don't you know how to use a bloody hammer girl? Hit it!" Sergeants. never swore at us and we all stopped and looked at him. There was silence for a few seconds, he probably thought we would down tools. Whatever his thoughts he threw off his tunic, rolled up his sleeves, took the hammer from the girl and proceeded to demonstrate how a hammer should be swung to break rocks. Considering none of us had ever done anything remotely like road-making before, it was surely expecting rather a lot to imagine that we could turn into navvies overnight. Even if we knew what to do, we weren't capable of swinging heavy hammers shoulder high and splitting boulders with ease. It was all some of us could do to pick the hammers up at all: we compromised by holding them down near the bottom of the shaft and dropping them down on the stones. Another day a hot and angry girl was standing beside her upturned barrow which had spilled its load as soon as she started to push it. "Damn!" she announced (with arms akimbo) in a loud voice to us all, including an officer who was watching from a safe distance, "If I can't have any babies when this war is over I shall sue the army!"

Fortunately, this all happened about July during a spell of dry weather, so the work both on the gun emplacements and the roadways was duly completed to everyone's satisfaction. It was a long time before our hands recovered from the blisters and abrasions though. If there hadn't been a war on, a soak in a hot bath would have been taken to soothe away the aches and pains. There was a war on and a hot bath was a rarity. ATS baths, for the use of, had a mark painted round, five inches from the bottom and we were honour bound not to fill above this mark. There were two baths, sections used them on alternate days and each hut organised its own roster. Of course you didn't always get hot water.

Laundry was collected and delivered once a fortnight, the ATS did some of their own because there was a drying room on Freddy site; not all sites were equipped with one. In Stockton we discovered a Chinese laundry, from then on we took our shirts and loose collars there. ATS shirts were worn with back and front studs just the same as the men's.

Rags were used for cleaning the guns and there were never enough, so the ATS would be sent in pairs to the houses near the site sometimes to beg for rags. They were fairly large houses, some kept maids who would answer the door in cap and apron. We certainly experienced a variety of tasks never envisaged while training as gunners. Imagine our folly in thinking that all our time would be spent on guns, instruments, marching and the lecture room, when manning a gunsite.

We got to know one of the maids quite well, she was a kind girl and invited us to visit her home which was some miles beyond Stockton. She was allowed a day and a night every week at home. We told her that we wouldn't like her job and she said she wouldn't like ours. Three of us went home with her one week, Urquhart, Stevenson and I were on 24-hours' leave together. Molly liked dancing too and a dance was being held that night in the village. Molly's family gave us a warm welcome and insisted we stayed the night, enabling us all to go to the dance and stay for the last waltz. Spare beds were usually available in households, sons belonging to many of them away in one of the services. It was like being at home in one way for me, a village dance with all the same ingredients. Everyone knew everyone else except for we three and a sprinkling of other uniforms. A three-piece band and a variety of ages, very young, mature, older and elderly. We enjoyed a friendly relationship with the local people and found much warmth and kindness in the north.

To get to Stockton from the site meant a ten minute walk along to a crossroads where the bus terminus was and the built up area began. A bus did pass the site on its way from Darlington to Stockton, but you still had to catch it at the crossroads. Only a few buses a day ran this service, but one ran in the early evening and, if you were lucky, the kindly bus drivers would stop and pick up a uniformed walker. The ATS widened a gap in the hedge a long way off from the main gate. We used this to wait, crouching out of sight of the gate in hope that the Darlington bus would stop for us. From hut 10, two or three of us would sneak out sometimes to go dancing, when not on manning duty and when we'd finished cookhouse fatigues for the day. It was worth it if only for an hour and a half of music and dance, we considered; that's all it would amount to, for we were always back in time for Roll Call. Not all the girls dared or wished to risk the consequences, only three in our hut were dance-mad as they called it. We were fully confident that no one would report our escapades, such was the comradeship that had grown among us and although they grumbled, as the whole hut would be punished if we were caught, loyalty prevailed.

Girls coming from such varied homes and backgrounds didn't always see eye to eye on every occasion, far from it, and were not slow in stating their opinions. Because of our fairly enclosed lifestyle, however, differences got thrashed out as and when they cropped up. As in a large family, each had their say, nothing was left to smoulder and all grievances were aired. Lack of privacy was something we all had to get used to but we gained, I am sure, more than we lost.

Once or twice the quick change from fatigue dress to service dress and the wait in the shelter of the hedge turned out to be fruitless, for the bus didn't stop. Fortunately, most of the bus drivers seemed to enjoy aiding and abetting the truants, but the first time it happened we said a few unkind words about that particular driver. What to do next?

"Well" I said, "I'll go back in and see who is on sentry duty."

"You can't walk through the site in service dress," Stevenson pointed out, "ask one of the others to go and look." The male guard would have taken over by that time and though there was a fairly good rapport between men and girls, it would be out of the question to ask one of them to look the other way while three ATS skulked past the main gate. We knew the ones likely to be eagle eyed and the ones who would just be standing in the sentry box in body only, their mind elsewhere till something approached the gate.

"And then what?" said Urquhart. "It will be too late to go dancing even if we manage to catch a bus at the terminus."

"Well, I said again, "ask the others if they would like some chips and we could pass the gate on the other side of the road one at a time, then we could walk down past the crossroads and look for a chip shop." After we'd reached agreement on that, Stevenson crept back through the hedge to ask one of our hut mates to check who was on guard. Yes they would all love some chips and when the one checking the guard said we should risk it, Stevenson collected cash from each and crawled through the hedge again.

"We had better find some chips after all this palaver," she grumbled. "I'm beginning to wonder if it's worth it."

"Come on, come on!" I chivvied her. "Where's your spirit of adventure?" We slipped quietly past the gate walking on the grass verge and, luckily, found a chip shop open not too far from the crossroads. On our return safely through the hedge and nearing our hut, we met an ATS Sergeant from D section. Perhaps she wouldn't realise that we hadn't an evening pass. A vain hope; of course she did.

"Oh yes," she said, "what have we here?" the three of us inwardly groaned.

"Chips," this from Urquhart.

"Give me a few, then I won't remember that I've seen you," said the Sergeant. If it had been our Sergeant it would have meant trouble indeed, serious trouble. As it was, we spent a few uncomfortable days wondering whether the axe would fall, not being sure how good was her word. Doling out the chips inside the hut, we related the incident to the others. "I knew you would get caught one night you little devils!" said Hunt who was the eldest one in the hut, all of twenty nine. Her profession in civilian life was a Nanny, trained by one of the best Nursemaid establishments in London. Much of the time she treated us like children, but on occasions could be as different again and laugh with the rest of us over some happening or other. It was she of the shrapnel episode and we never dared mention it in her hearing, though she would share in a joke against another girl. We always found something to joke about, it was a way of coping. Even if you were the butt of the merriment, the bitter pill of humiliation was coated by the fact that the laughter was mainly good humoured and that it would be someone else's turn next time. All of us, well nearly all of us, had acquired an ability to laugh at ourselves.

For a few weeks after being caught we didn't dare go through the hedge, but our courage returned and we continued as before. At the end of Tarrant Street was a church, and dances were held in the hall next to it. We used to pass a chip shop on the way to the bus after dashing out of the dance. Sometimes we'd go in for chips if there wasn't much of a queue. One night in the chip shop we got chatting to a girl dressed in Fire Service uniform. She said that she only lived a few doors away and invited us for a cup of tea. Her mother had the kettle on and made us welcome, the Firewoman had just come off duty. We only had time for a quick cup of tea before catching the bus, but they invited us to spend our next 24-hr pass with them. The son was in the Royal Navy and we took it in turns to write to him. We spent some pleasant hours with that family and Molly's too; they were kind people sharing their fireside with us so far from our own. We missed them all when we moved from Freddy site. We met with kindness in nearly all the places we were stationed during our years in uniform.

Old Soldiers

Stockton-on-Tees was well supplied with places to eat (always high on our list of priorities), places to dance and several cinemas. We had a favourite restaurant which, in spite of rationing, still managed to provide the most delicious cakes. We wallowed in luxury sitting in its comfortable surroundings at a table spread with damask and china. The hum of chatter from other tables, the tinkling of cups and the cakestand placed on the table before us, was sheer bliss. Twenty-four hours away from the site re-charged our batteries. It was such a complete change from bare floors, wooden-topped tables and benches, thick enamel mugs, plain food, tea served from buckets and the same faces day in, day out in a khaki world.

One of the duties of the Orderly Officer was to visit the other ranks' dining room to see if there were any complaints about the food. I don't remember if anyone ever did complain; another important thing we had learned during training was never to complain about the food for it wouldn't make the slightest scrap of difference. The ATS especially avoided doing so in front of an officer or an NCO knowing the stock answer would be "You're in the army now." A Sergeant once told me that when he was in a male battery, an officer said to a gunner who did complain about a surfeit of beans, "Don't you know that a man can march a mile on a bean?" The Globe Cinema in Stockton was where four of us ate our way through a few pounds of plums one summer afternoon while watching Clark Gable, Leslie Howard and Vivien Leigh in *Gone With The Wind*. The film ran for three hours. Although we couldn't buy sweets, when fruit was in season we'd buy that to munch while watching films. Fruit grown in the British Isles was all there was available, so out of season we did without. Other memorable films were *We Dive At Dawn, The Gentle Sex, Mrs. Minniver, White Christmas, Brief Encounter* with Trevor Howard and Celia Johnson and *The Wicked Lady* with James Mason and Margaret Lockwood. These films were enjoyed in the company of hut-mates unless in a cosy twosome. Some girls had regular boyfriends away abroad in the desert or on the high seas and one or two were married or engaged. These would usually go out together on evening and 24-hr passes. The dancing trio would go to the cinema in the afternoon and dance in the evening. Not all stayed out at night on 24-hr passes. Some slept on site, it was cheaper, but unless we were broke we opted to stay away the whole 24 hours. The YMCA and YWCA provided a useful service for servicemen and women, with sleeping accommodation for short periods.

Whatever your aches and pains, whatever malady (real or imagined) you were suffering from, if your name was on Battery Orders for a pass, then a miraculous cure took place. On site there was a medical orderly for the men and one for the ATS. A medical officer (MO) if needed was at Regimental HQ. Once a month everyone on site was given a Free From Infection (FFI) test. If anyone was suspected of suffering from anything infectious, then the whole lot of us were checked. An annual injection of TAB (Typhoid -paratyphoid A and B) and one of TT (Tuberculin-tested) were given to each of us. Dental care was attended to at an army Dental Centre, the patient was escorted there by one of the medical orderlies.

One morning I woke up with a sore throat. We didn't report sick unless we were at death's door so this didn't bother me too much, but I began to feel worse during the morning. I was on a 24-hr pass starting at 2 p.m. though, so the thought of that kept me going. After spending some time in Stockton, we had arranged to have a meal then catch a bus to Ferryhill where Molly lived; she would be already at home. We were spending the night there, needless to say we were all going dancing. While they were all getting ready to go to the dance that evening, styling each other's hair with a pair of old-fashioned curling tongs, I felt too rotten to be interested. There was an aroma of singed hair mixed with Phulnana perfume which they were all sharing. I was wishing they would hurry up and go. When I told them that I was just going to sit by the fire for a little while then go to bed, they realised that I must be ill and suggested taking it in turns to sit with me. I thanked them and said I'd rather be left alone, my head was thumping. Molly's mother made me a hot drink with something in it out of the kitchen cupboard and they all went gaily off to the dance.

Although I said that I felt much better the next morning, I really felt much worse. I was certainly not looking forward to manning duty on the Command Post that afternoon. You needed all your wits about you even when the air attack was only a simulated one and I hoped there wouldn't be an alarm that night. I got through the day without making any blunders but the following morning I couldn't get out of bed. Someone brought me a mug of tea back from breakfast, but I had a job to swallow it. I was reported sick and the medical orderly said she hoped no one had been giving me hot tea to send up my temperature. As if tea carried from a bucket in the dining hall that cold winter morning would be anything other than lukewarm! The medical orderly diagnosed tonsillitis and said that the MO would have to confirm it. If it was tonsillitis then I would be going to the Military Hospital. In the meantime I was to get dressed and stay in the hut until the MO came. This seemingly harsh treatment, unusual for McInnes who resided in our hut, was because she had just that morning been informed from Battery Office about a visit. Apparently, a party of young girl cadets of some kind were visiting the site that morning to be shown how attractive the life of ATS on gunsites was! On the nine o'clock parade the ATS were warned, well threatened, not to paint a black picture of our career in uniform, or dire retribution would follow. The recruiting for girls on gunsites was slowing down to a trickle and visits like these might help spark off some enthusiasm, it was considered.

The officers need not have worried one jot about their girl gunners letting the side down; pride was to the fore as always; none of us would tell of our sometimes unhappier moments to an outsider. In any case the one doubtful C section member who may have slipped a grumble in was silenced by the fact that she'd lost her voice and wasn't capable of taking part in anything going on around her. A false note was introduced which we thought silly, two girls from each hut were sent to make all the beds in the ATS huts. It wasn't allowed to make beds before afternoon duties were over except those on 24-hr passes after 2 p.m. parade. They could if they wished, stay in them till the next morning but would have to get out and fold blankets like the rest before hut inspection. I suppose the bare-looking tidy Nissen huts did look a shade more inviting with the beds made, but if the possible recruits were expecting comfort then they wouldn't volunteer for Ack Ack, they'd join the WRNS.

The chambermaids went away, the cadets came in with an ATS NCO who ignored me as if I was part of the furniture. This suited me, I wasn't up to explanations. As the party were going out of the hut the MO came in, and shortly after that the ambulance came. I was carted from the bed "looking like a little owl all hunched up with her greatcoat round her" was how one stretcher bearer put it. Goodness knows how many cadets I had infected by then. No matter, the RAMC carefully placed me in an ambulance wrapped in cosy red blankets and off we went. If I hadn't felt so ill I'd have enjoyed the stay in hospital, the warmth, the lovely bed, the fluffy blankets and a hot water bottle to cuddle. I was glad to be better, but a day or two longer would have been acceptable. No convalescence though, back to duty for me to find nothing had changed. I slipped back into my place, a little cog in a large wheel.

On the whole we were a healthy lot, there was no VD in either sex and only a very few reported sick unless they really were. The ATS, of course, were all A1 and sound in wind and limb – the men were a different kettle of fish. Medical Records, and all things pertaining to, were naturally top secret. It wasn't until after the war that I received the information about the health situation. The Royal Artillery manned guns on merchant ships; one Sergeant in the battery had served on board these ships and had been torpedoed more than once before being posted to us. One suffered badly from shell shock – he was put on non-operational duties. Some of the older ones were low in health grades and were never sent overseas. These men had regular check-ups to see how they were coping, of course all this was known only to the CO and the medical staff.

I think there were only two pregnancies the whole time. That state could never remain a secret in our circumstances, although there is always the exception and the exception did occur. I don't think our medical orderly ever quite recovered from the fact that, until the birth was imminent within seconds, she did not suspect. How on earth the girl had managed to conceal it remained a mystery. What made things worse was the fact that she took ill in the night and the MO couldn't be reached. A doctor from the Royal Navy was called and his awesome words were "This girl is giving birth, that's all that's wrong with her." The girl said it must be an immaculate conception! That happened long after we'd moved from Freddy site when we had acquired Radar and GL girls. The girl in question was a GL girl and they were a law unto themselves. Suffice it to say that some of their equipment was so advanced that many RA officers knew little about it, which put them at a disadvantage. For whatever reason they lived a little apart from the rest of us, working entirely different shifts. They didn't do guard duty, cookhouse fatigues or any of the menial tasks in our daily lives. An ATS GL Sergeant ruled over their domain. Our paths didn't cross very often but when they did, we found them human, the same as us, and got on well with them. The instrument they manned was part of the whole system and if they had been trained as well as the rest of us, then the operational side of the gunsite was the main thing and all that really mattered.

While we were on F site, Germany carried out what it called reprisal raids on the cathedral cities of England – Canterbury, Bath, Exeter, York, Norwich and Coventry. All but Coventry were for the most part undefended. For a while we were not so active in the north and although the site was always kept up to a high state or readiness, minds and bodies alert through constant training and exercise, the Sergeants. it seemed, were finding the lack of combat a trifle boring. They cast around for some form of diversion, namely us. Not in the more usual sense though. We were gunners and had to be treated as such, in some respects we were subjected to harsher treatment than the male gunners. Sex equality existed long before the hullaballoo in later years. The ATS went through a period where one or more of us were always being given extra fatigues for one thing or another, inmates of certain huts given extra marching drill in the evenings on some pretext. Sometimes we were marched up and down outside the gate on the Darlington Road by one of the male Sergeants in the evening. It was unusual and not on Battery Orders, but ours not to reason why, if an order was given then we carried it out. This uneasy sate of affairs went on for some time.

One evening, seven or eight of us were sent down to the cookhouse, after normal duties were finished, to clean a pile of old black cooking tins. The method was to use ash from the boiler to try and restore the tins to pristine condition, a nigh impossible task. As soon as we were all busy outside the cookhouse, some of us working on the table and some sitting on the ground, one of our number said she had something important to tell us. We all stopped scrubbing and listened. The Orderly corporal in charge listened too. One of the orderlies in the Sergeants' Mess had overheard some RA Sergeants discussing a wager. It seemed they had been laying bets as to how many ATS they could put on extra fatigues and marching drill after normal duties, for the flimsiest of reasons. We discussed this at great length as we rubbed the tins. The conclusion we came to was to carry on and not give the Sergeants the satisfaction of seeing us get rattled. The suggestion that we should tell the only ATS officer on site was turned down, of course the Sergeants would deny it and we might fare worse in the long run.

The evening turned into a noisy one, we sang, we laughed and thought of schemes of revenge, all of which were sheer fantasy. A number of the others had drifted down to discover the cause of the hilarity and they helped us to put away the fruits of our labours. Naturally they were told about the wager, melting away as the Orderly Corporal came back to say she'd informed the Orderly Sergeant that we'd finished the tins. He told the corporal to march us to the parade square and stand us in line to attention. Then he went along the line asking each girl in turn if she knew why she had been given extra fatigues pointing to each girl as he asked.

The first in line answered, "Because I didn't hear the whistle Sergeant." He went along asking the same question and getting the same answer till he came to the last girl in line, she answered, "Because I was late on parade Sergeant." The rest of us must have had a mental blockage for us to repeat parrot fashion the first girl's silly answer. During that day we had been about two seconds late on dinner parade, hence the cookhouse tins. The Sergeant dismissed the last girl and told the corporal to march the rest of us back to the cookhouse for another quarter of an hour. She, her wrath by this time boiling over, carried out the order. Telling us to stay there, she went in high dudgeon to find the Orderly Officer. We looked at each other then one said, "Do you think she has gone to tell about the bets?" "What else?" I answered and the bravest one among us said with a large grin, "I don't think we ought to miss this do you? Come on!" With comments of "in for a penny, in for a pound" and "you only die once," we trooped after the corporal.

As the Orderly Officer came out of the Mess to speak to the corporal, we stopped a little way behind her. He glared at us, his relaxing evening in the Mess disturbed by those dratted ATS, returned the corporal's salute and said, "Yes what is it Corporal?" She proceeded to tell him what she'd heard about the wager and the evening fatigues. He roared as only that man could roar, said it was mutiny and if we didn't get back to the cookhouse immediately, we would all be charged with it. Faced with that, what else was there to do? Discretion being the better part of valour we went, smarting with the injustice of it just the same. No one had anything to say on the way back, but the minute we turned the corner of the cookhouse and out of sight, we collapsed over the table in gales of laughter. Blessed, relieving, releasing of tension, laughter. Somehow through the bad times, the sad times, when in a group, it only needed a look or a word to spark it off.

After the allocated quarter of an hour at the cookhouse, the corporal came to dismiss us. She told us that the Orderly

Officer had threatened her with court martial if it all turned out to be false. We had calmed down a bit by then, fortunately, as the corporal didn't look too happy. ATS corporals tended to stand up for the girls even if the ATS Sergeants didn't stick their necks out. I suppose sharing the Mess with RA Sergeants they had to tread warily.

A day or two after the incident the corporal was sent to G site on some pretext or other. She couldn't understand why she was there at all and put in more than one request to be returned to F site. We also asked when she was coming back, she had been a popular girl and we hoped there wouldn't be a replacement from G site; "better the devil you know" and all that.

The Sergeants appeared to have let up a bit on the extra marching and evening fatigues, though to be honest I didn't mind extra marching at all. The corporal was eventually returned to the fold and, by degrees, information filtered through to us about the "storm in a teacup". The officer had looked into the matter of the betting Sergeants. Whether all of them were involved or just some of them, we never found out. One of them spilled the beans and had been threatening to make trouble for the corporal, so she was removed from the scene of friction for a spell until things had cooled down a little, thereby avoiding a situation that may have split the ranks. That is all we discovered and were ever likely to. It all blew over and the incident was relegated to the list of anecdotes to be mulled over at some later date on one of the many sessions round the hut fire before and after lights out. After lights out, sessions were only possible when the hut corporal was on a course or on leave.

On-site entertainment was the odd concert or two from ENSA held in the NAFFI and one which we produced ourselves. The Chocolate Soldier, for some reason, was always sung in all the ENSA concerts we ever had. They were all appreciated whatever they sang. We had a few musicians among our ranks so our concert was made up of individual items and ended with a sing song. Later we managed to improve on that format using a little more imagination. On that first home-produced concert though, an ATS Sergeant named Sue did use some imagination for her spot. Only she knew what was in her imagination though, none of the rest of us did. Music from a record was playing as she came on to the stage wearing weird make-up, her face with a greenish hue and heavily mascara'd eyes. She was dressed in ragged strips of flimsy material; dressed was an exaggeration, for when she danced or moved her body to the music, it appeared that she might end up undressed. By the hoots and whistles from the male part of the audience, it was clear they hoped she would. Suddenly she threw up her arms, jumped off the makeshift stage and ran down the centre aisle emitting loud terrifying screeches and out through the door. A few desultory claps were heard but from the rest a stunned silence. No one seemed to know whether the last bit had been part of the act or not, her fellow Sergeants didn't know as she'd kept her act a secret. The bombardier acting as MC announced the next turn and the concert went on. One of the ATS Sergeants slipped out when the lights dimmed, presumably to check that the star was all right, and came back in a few minutes. A few in the front row wearing "pips," visibly relaxed and we all settled down to enjoy the remaining items. The spell had been broken though and everyone seemed glad when the show ended and the NAAFI staff opened their shutters for what was left of the evening. We never held another concert on Freddy site and by the time we did venture to tread the boards again, the spectacular Sergeant had left us.

One day a contingent of smart but somewhat elderly figures in khaki marched on to the site. They were the local Home Guard on a visit to see how a gunsite operated. If truth be known the information that interested them mainly was how did a gunsite operate with females who weren't in the kitchen or other accepted areas, but near guns beside the men. They spent the morning with us and were shown the rest of the site, cookhouse, huts, ablutions, as well as watching the manning teams in practice. D section were manning, so we in C section did not get the chance to show our efficiency on Command Post drill. The Home Guard used the NAAFI at break time and though one or two looked at the ATS as if they thought we might bite, they ended up chatting with us. One said he had a daughter who looked like me but he could never imagine her

Above The first day at Arborfield Barracks for 536 (Mixed) Heavy Ack Ack Battery. Left to right: Struggles, Thomson, Stevenson

Below Astley Pool, one of the local landscapes I particularly missed during the early days at Arborfield.

Above F-Site, our first gunsite. From back, left-right: Atterton, Crisp, MacInnes, Hague, Urquhart, Amy, Wellsbury, Stevenson, Ivy, Thomson.

Right Podge ready for
the egg run.

Left Vee Thomson wearing the
badge of the Royal Artillery

*Right:*Thomson,
Urquhart and Stevenson
in the mock fur 'teddy'
coveralls issued to Ack
Ack sites in the winter
1942.

Left Atterton and Thomson hunting for sticks.

Right Ash and elbow grease: Thomson and Jackson on jankers.

Left Thomson and Urquhart just when we thought we were finished.

Right Urquhart, Cpl Crisp, Thomson with the tomahawk. It was not much good for chopping wood, but Hague killed a mouse with it one night!.

Left Cpl Kay Crisp married Harold Reed, RAF.

Above The Landgate, Rye where we rattled through on a trailer to be landgirls.

Below 'X' marks the spot: our billet in Market Street.

Above Remaining few of 536 await their fate, among them: MacInnes, Amy, Hague, Thomson, Stevenson and Urquhart.

Right Vee Thomson marries George Sydney Robinson, RE, 1947.

Above The September 1989 reunion was held at Rosyln castle. Some came for the day, but others spent a week together.

Below Return to our gunsite position beside the Forth Bridge in 1989. From the left: Urquhart, Hague, MacInnes, Crisp, Stevenson, Thomson.

near a gun. I think they were a little surprised to find that we were treated the same as the men without any concessions usually afforded to the fairer sex. Whether the visit was an army Public Relations exercise or not I don't know, it never happened again and was the only time civilians were allowed on site.

Stevenson and I on fatigues one day were ordered to clean the sleeping quarters of two of the RA Sergeants. This was unheard of, but it was an order so we obeyed. The hut was the same size as ours which slept twelve, but only two of them shared it. Sergeants didn't have to fold their blankets, nor did the hut appear to have been cleaned in the recent past. We had assumed that the Sergeants' quarters would be cleaned by the male gunners on fatigues if we thought about it at all, yet I was never told to clean an ATS Sergeants room. The place, we told each other, was a pigsty, surely they didn't like living in such squalor?

I said to my fellow skivvy, my mind harking back to events past, "Do you think they've left it like this on purpose?"

"Probably, surely they wouldn't choose to live like the pigs those two are," Stevenson said. She laughed and added, "I don't know though, it's probably all they're used to."

"Right then," I said "let's give it the spring-clean of a lifetime."

Stevenson answered, "If you intend to do that it will take us a lifetime."

We set to with a will. When the task was completed we stood back and surveyed our handiwork with satisfaction. It had the woman's touch we thought. The filthy lathered shaving mugs were scoured and filled with wild flowers from the hedge, the two beds were made hospital-fashion, all corners tucked in, the floor as spotless as we could make it. Windows cleaned, clothes folded and put away. It would pass inspection even by the dust-obsessed officer. We had added one or two personal touches of our own just to finish off, like sewing up pyjama legs and arms and making apple pie beds with a few leaves and stones inside the folded sheets. We thought of a few more ideas but time was against us and we decided it might be unwise to add any more.

For the next few days the pair of us waited with not exactly fear and trepidation, but a little apprehension as to what form of repercussion would assail us. It was quite some time before we stopped expecting any. As far as I know, never again were ATS ordered to clean RA Sergeants sleeping quarters.

Another little ripple stirred our pond of fairly smooth water one day, when Stevenson and I were again on fatigues together. This time we were ordered to the Officers' Mess to do the cleaning. Normally they had their own orderlies and batmen, but that day some of them were on leave or sick. It wasn't sleeping quarters but the dining hall and kitchen we were to clean, duties to include laying the table for meals. This was all straightforward as far as we were concerned and made a change. Just slightly higher class than the lower ranks' surroundings but still fatigues, dressed in our shapeless, unflattering, denim apology for a uniform.

Our hackles rose when we were informed that we'd be required to wait at table and to proceed forthwith to stores to collect white overalls! We were in the kitchen when this bombshell was dropped and two more things dropped as we threw the vegetable knives we both wielded into the sink with a clatter. Silence reigned for about two seconds then I found my voice. "Come on Stevenson," and we both ran out of the kitchen.

"I'm not waiting on officers," said Stevenson, "but what are we going to do?"

"We are certainly not going to wait on table for one thing, whether it means a court martial or not," I answered with passion. "We," laying emphasis on the we, "have been trained at great expense to be operational and though we are obliged to do the necessary chores on site for the smooth running of it, no one can change our status, we are gunners."

"Yes, all right," agreed Stevenson, "but who are you going to say all that to?"

"Well," I pondered, "Darkie Day is Orderly Sergeant so he won't be on the Command Post. Come on let's find him, he knows Kings Rules and Regulations off by heart."

We found Sergeant Day and he confirmed that no one could force us to wait on the officers at table but we could volunteer he told us, knowing as he said it with a twinkle in his eye that there wasn't much chance of that happening. "Go back to the mess and carry on with what you were doing," he said, "and I'll see the ATS Sergeant, but you'll stay on for the 24 hours as detailed. No you won't be doing waitress service," as he saw us getting ready for an argument, "off you go at the double." We returned to our vegetables and carried on quietly having lived to fight another day. We finished the whole stint quietly in fact and thankfully resumed manning duties at the end of it. That was another "detail" we never found ourselves on again.

Fires in huts were sanctioned from October 1st up until the end of April. The allowance per day per hut was three parts of a bucket full of coke, this to be collected daily by one member from each hut, from a wired enclosure kept locked and in charge of the boilerman. The fuel could be collected at 4 p.m.; our hut took it in turns. The black iron stove sat in the middle of the hut defying us to light it. Confidently, two of the girls set about the task, they had never tried to light a belligerent antiquity like that before, neither had they or any of us tried to light a fire with coke. After nearly all of us except the ones getting ready for their evening leave had tried without a flicker of flame, we had to give up. By the time this happened though, the evening was half gone. It was a noisy session, one rattling the stovepipe chimney saying it must be full of soot, two others arguing about the amount of paper one had put in the bottom. Another said we needed some hot passionate love letters to start a blaze and had anyone got any. In the middle of the noisy scene Odgers came in, no one had noticed her departure, she held in her hands a bundle of sticks, her rosy face beamed. "Don't ask any questions," she said, "and don't think it will happen again because it won't, I nearly promised my honour for these."

We did have a fire that night and from then on all those going out of camp were duty bound to hunt for firewood from any source. On our way to the crossroads for the bus, we'd scour the hedgerows under the trees for every twig and hide them till we could collect them on the way back, not always easy in the pitch dark. The fire in our hearth not only gave warmth to our bodies but warmth to our spirits. The lucky ones with beds nearest the stove sat on them, the rest dragged kit boxes around in a circle, writing letters, signing, mending, reading or just talking. Sitting dressed in identical striped flannelette pyjamas, wearing greatcoats round our shoulders, we discoursed on the past, the future, the present. On people, on love and life, on our beliefs and on eternity. Some of the talk was nonsense, some profound and all of it was beneficial. The discussions about romances, our own or anyone else's, were not gone into deeply, though very much talked of, no intimacies were disclosed. No one expected to be told, neither did anyone tell.

Hunt (nicknamed Nan), was the one who'd been a Nanny. Tall with brown hair, she had been engaged to a sailor, but sadly he was lost at sea when his ship was torpedoed. Nan belonged to Bournemouth and found the north cold and bleak. Atterton (nicknamed Natterton), came from Norfolk and had an amusing way of phrasing things. Her name was Edna but she was never called by it, she would say "Where be you now going?" but it didn't sound like that when he said it. She was tall with brown hair, big brown eyes and was engaged to an air force boy. Gunner Amy (Christian name Dorothy) was a tall girl with brown hair and brown eyes and came from Ipswich. McInnes, Grace, the medical orderly, didn't start out as a medical orderly though, but as a Predictor Number. While we were at Arborfield it was realised that a medical orderly would be needed for the ATS in our half of the battery so Grace was asked to change over to that duty. She refused at first, she had, like the rest of us, volunteered for operational duty and wanted to do just that. Some heavy persuasion followed with the possibility of half the battery being minus the services of a medical orderly for the ATS, so being a softhearted caring person, she agreed to accept the post. Her fiancé was a soldier in one of the highland regiments and was a prisoner of war. Again, she was a tall girl, as was Corporal Crisp – hut 10 had a good half of the chorus line among its members. Crisp (nicknamed Chips), Doris her real name, was Hut Corporal and sorry sometimes that it was our hut she was in. Her hometown was Reigate, she had an airman too. Odgers or Podge (first name Peggy, hence the nickname), was from Cornwall. With a strange Cornish charm, she never seemed to get into any trouble somehow. Rosy cheeks, light brown short curly hair, blue eyes and beaming smile, she sailed her way through our sometimes stormy passage without ever being caught up in any of it. Her charm enabled her to evade unpleasant fatigues or extra duties.

Podge and the four others were all younger and smaller than the rest, between five foot nothing and five foot one and half inches. None of them had a steady boyfriend so they could have fun and play the field. Stevenson (christened Dorothy), did have a sort of an understanding with a boy from her home in Staffordshire, but that didn't get serious till much later on, he was an airman too. Stevenson was a fairly quiet girl except when roused. Urquhart from Glasgow (name of Margaret), fiery in spasms, but laughed a lot. Hague from Birmingham (christened Nora Eunice and she never forgave her parents for this), also laughed at lot, had rosy cheeks and fair, short, wavy hair. She was handy for doing little jobs around the hut when a strong hand was needed and was as nosy as the rest in an argument.

Then there was Thomson without the P. Blonde and blue-eyed, not chocolate-box-lid type and definitely not as sweet as the contents of a chocolate box. If there was any trouble I was likely to be in it, or at least on the fringe. A fair assortment of girls who would never have met under normal circumstances.

One evening round the stove, the chatter was about the differences between us and we decided to discuss these at length. It couldn't be expected that thrown together as we were in such a close environment, harmony would reign at all times. Through the months of training and the excitement of being operational the momentum was continuous, but when life settled down into just routine, some things were irksome with minor irritations. The winter weather we found harsh, out in most of it either on Command Post, Guard duty or cleaning vegetables outside the cookhouse. The warmth inside when doing the washing up was welcome and we were glad to be inside a lecture hut however boring the subject.

The hut fire was an important part of our well-being. As we sat round it that particular evening, it was on a serious note. Someone suggested that we each write down a list of our known faults. This we did in silence, most unusual for a hut fire session. When we had all finished writing, the next suggestion was that we each read out our list and the others would add to it, if in the opinion of them the list wasn't complete. We knew each other well enough by that time to know that no offence was intended and none would be taken. The lists and additions were completed to the satisfaction of all, not without laughter of course. Then each of us stood in turn and ceremoniously dropped the list into the flames. I can't remember what we intoned as we did this, but do doubt we thought it fitting for the occasion. It was something to the effect that we would correct all our faults from that moment. We all were sincere and for a time tried hard, but human nature is not perfect and neither were the ATS in hut 10.

Christmas 1942, the Eighth Army were advancing towards Tripoli over desolate sand dunes. British women were thinking of their menfolk in all the war zones and trying their best to celebrate Christmas for the sake of the children in spite of the shortages of every commodity. On Freddy site the ATS officer announced that there would be a decorated hut competition for the ATS. She didn't give this information till a few days before Christmas so there wasn't much time to either plan or forage for the wherewithal to decorate the huts. The ones with a 24-hr pass were detailed to buy whatever they could, the rest of us to do the labour. We couldn't plan until we knew what there was available, plenty of brilliant ideas were put forward, but how to execute them was another thing.

There wasn't a wood within miles and apart from the fine specimens in some of the gardens along the road, no evergreen trees within our reach. One of our green-fingered members had planted two bowls of daffodils and luckily they were already in bud. The shoppers didn't have much luck. With red crepe paper we dressed the stove up to resemble a pillar box, the bowls of daffodils looked beautiful and with our array of Christmas cards it was the best we could do. Everyone was made to suffer for the sake of art, one night without a hut fire because the judging was to take place the next morning. I can't remember what the prize was but we won! The honour was the thing, C Section hut 10.

Christmas day on a gunsite in wartime was not much different to any other day, morning parades, drills and fatigues were carried out. We marched to the dining hall and were served in army tradition by the officers, it was all a bit unreal. If the officers hadn't been present, I think there may have been a little more hilarity. As it was, apart from a better than usual dinner, it was not all that joyful. I suppose we were thinking of other things that Christmas day in uniform while we kept watch, not over "flocks by night" but skywards for enemy raiders. At night round the stove, divested of its trappings, we sang carols. On the whole it was rather a quiet evening, each of us thinking of loved ones, wishing for a magic carpet to fly home for just a little while and wondering where we would be next Christmas.

North Of The Border

Efficient as the teams were in practice and in action, it was considered by the higher echelon that batteries needed a spell of continuous firing practice now and again, if not provided for by the enemy. Off to a firing camp went the whole battery for four weeks of further training. This time to a safer spot, the west coast of Scotland.

Burrowhead was a rough piece of moorland, wild and windy, nothing much there but a few sheep and some well-hidden huts. The guns as in Norfolk were sited on the edge of the cliffs and much higher and wilder was the whole area. A long winding road led from the camp to a tiny little harbour with a few fishing boats. The Isle of Whithorn, so called, had a pub and a few cottages. Evening passes were more frequent, but it was such a long trek down to the pub where toasted cheese and sandwiches could be devoured and half pints of shandy quaffed, that we seldom left the shelter of our huts. Added to that the gate was such a long way out of sight of the huts you needed a map reference to find it. Very far away from civilisation, a perfect place for training, just acres of nothing. Everywhere entailed a route march, sleeping huts in one place, dining hall miles away, lecture rooms somewhere else, latrines nowhere near anything at all. The canteen was run by the Church of Scotland and Church Parade was held there.

The huts were decidedly grubby, the "biscuits" on the two-tier bunks were suspect and a few days after our arrival a number of the ATS reported to the Medical Inspection (MI) room with infestations which turned out to be scabies. Great was the consternation among our ranks and confrontation between our officers and those of the permanent staff must have been heated, to say the least. Ours insisting that we had been infected after arrival at the camp, their opposite numbers insisting with equal indignation that we must have brought them with us. Then a day or so later, to their horror, some girls discovered they had head lice as well. A lot of time was spent in the MI room by the unfortunate ones for treatment sessions. The rest of us were examined from head to toe at regular intervals during the month.

The daily training went on much as before on gun park and in lecture room. As before, another battery was training at the same time as we were. One day a list of names chalked up on the Command Post appeared, courtesy of "nobody". Whoever it was, the ones so named were ordered to remove it and we were marched up after tea with buckets of water and scrubbing brushes. Rather unfair we grumbled, as if anyone would be stupid enough to scrawl their own names.

Dances were held in camp twice a week and there was a camp cinema – well, a wooden hut with wooden benches. We saw some good films in that wooden hut. For a month we'd enjoyed time free from cookhouse fatigues, guard duties, wheelbarrows and cleaning, apart from cleaning our huts. We had set about cleaning those before we unpacked, they looked a jolly sight cleaner when we left than when we arrived.

Back to the gunsites went the battery to carry on defending the skies after travelling by night on a long weary journey, setting out from Burrowhead when we would normally be going to bed. Troop trains never travelled by direct routes, we were never told when we would arrive anywhere. Glad to be back, going into our own hut was like going home, someone remarked.

The ATS were issued with another garment that winter, a kind of furry sack which you put on over your head. It laced up the front, with a hood, which was supposed to go over your hat leaving the cap badge visible and was for sentry duty only. Again the designer who was responsible for the PT kit and denims must have had a hand in the unflattering teddy-bear look. They were warm (no doubt about that), boots lined with the same material would have been welcome. They came in handy as an extra covering on the beds and for wearing over pyjamas when sitting round the stove.

Improvements for detecting enemy aircraft continued and one of the ATS Sergeants and Corporal Crisp were sent on a Plotting course. Radar was on its way to 536, a few sites only were equipped at the time. The sets were operated by ATS teams on a shift system round the clock; they scanned a small screen in a revolving cabin. Down beneath the Command Post, squashed in beside the telephonists, another ATS team would plot the aircraft on a plotting table with information relayed from the Radar screen.

It was the policy to switch batteries from one gunsite to another when they had served a certain length of time in one place, to prevent them from getting stale for one thing. Though all gunsites were the same basically, there could be differences in accommodation, recreation or sometimes in toilet facilities.

How much notice the Commanding Officer was given when a battery move was imminent I don't know, but the lower ranks only found out a couple of days before, when a small advance party was mustered. Consisting of both male and female gunners led by two Sergeants, they were responsible for taking over all equipment and accommodation from the departing battery on the new site. For a twenty-four-hour period the site would be out of action but the public never knew that.

We weren't officially told where or when we were moving, but a rumour was going round and rumours usually had a grain of truth in them. We were heading north and it would be colder seemed to be the general opinion. The Battery moved further north and it *was* cold. In wooden huts this time we all settled down again. Having windows on both sides instead of just at one end, the sleeping accommodation was much nicer but it was a long trek down a slope to the taps and wash basins for both girls and men.

HQ with A and B Sections was positioned on the end of the south side of the Forth Bridge, Sections C and D were to the west, three miles from the Firth of Forth. Actually, the former were manning the guns which had fired the first rounds of the war that day on September 19th when the first raiders appeared. Our guns were sited on farmland belonging to Merrilees Farm; Philipstoun was the map location but it was only a hamlet and some miles away.

Opposite the guardroom was a small copse, I loved this bit of woodland for two reasons; firewood could be gathered (one of our main concerns), and later when the trees were clothed in green it was pleasant to walk there. At the far end I used to stand and gaze at the view, trees and fields stretching as far as the eye could see. No electric pylons or factory chimneys to mar the scene and sometimes, on a sunny day when skies were quiet, members of our hut would go to the copse, chat as though on a country walk in peacetime and hold the silliest conversations. Some of us blessed with fertile imaginations would tell the wildest of stories as to why we were there in that wood at that particular time. Naturally, it was to take our minds off the war which affected our lives, home, families, hopes, dreams. We were all young enough to dream a lot.

The ground was uneven, humpty with hollows and hillocks, overgrown with brambles, a good place for hiding if you happened to be a German parachutist, we agreed. Having been well indoctrinated with security procedure from the beginning, the threat of possible invasion by parachute was never far from our minds, or the fact most probable that a German airman escaping from his plane hit by our guns might land in our vicinity. Thankfully, the Prowler Guard duties of the ATS had been discontinued before the move.

Outside the gate was a maze of winding country lanes not leading anywhere except to farms. The lane to the right of the gate however led down to a main road – a ten-minute walk – and was the only direction any of us took, except that is unless in a marching column. It was decided that each section would go on regular route marches *en bloc* with its own officer and NCOs. Most of us enjoyed this though there were a few of both sexes not as keen as the rest of us and who tried to dodge the exercise by various means. We sang all kinds of songs as we marched – old ones and current ones. Some good songs were written during the war, many being sentimental of course, but humorous ones too were written. Not all of them were suitable for marching to, but lots were. *The Quartermaster's Stores* was sung with varying words suitable for ATS, also *If You Want The Sergeant Major I know Where He Is*. If the men sang different words under their breath, no word untoward reached an ATS ear, and even though some of the gentler sex might know a few ungentle words, none was heard on those route marches. Predictor numbers made up their own words to the tune of *I Like to Ride The Ferry*. Not exactly Irving Berlin, but everyone joined in and it was heard being whistled or hummed from then on in the battery.

> *We love to man the Sperry*
> *when firing at a Jerry*
> *there's a noise just like*
> *a concertina*
> *when number one reports he's*
> *seen her.*
> *Eyes down Predictor steady*
> *fuse set the guns are ready*
> *when the order "Fire" goes*
> *the shell goes up and hits her nose*
> *one down we've hit a Dornier*
> *two down we'd better warn yer*
> *three down with the Sperry serenade.*

Another we sang to the tune of *Anchors Aweigh My Lads*.

> *We are the 536 marching along*
> *we are the ACK ACK girls and this is just our*
> *marching song*
> *we joined the Royal Artillery*
> *to fight for yours and mine*
> *and when we get to Germany we'll drown 'em in the,*
> *drown 'em in the Rhine.*

(The Sperry mark 11 was the type of Predictor we were using then.)

The Sight of men and girls wearing battledress winging along those country lanes and singing at the tops of their voices would have boosted the morale of the British public, but apart from cattle, sheep and a farm worker or two, no one saw us. We were fit, if we hadn't been, those marches would have resulted in some of us being invalided out. We marched wearing respirators in the usual position, steel helmets on the left shoulder, gas capes in rolled position at the back of the neck. After a certain number of miles, the order to halt and fall out was given for a ten minute break. Everyone flopped down on the verge, some even had enough breath left to puff a cigarette and there was always a field wall or some bushes available. A girl one day jumped over a wall without first looking, a squeal was heard and when others rushed to investigate they found the ground sloped steeply down from the wall. The girl only got a fright; she was lucky, there might have been a pond at the bottom.

Our shoulder flashes were still Northern Command, the red sword and scales of justice on a blue background. Eventually all Ack Ack personnel wore the same black bow and arrow on a red ground. The ATS much preferred the sword and scales but consoled themselves with the motto they wore, Ubique (everywhere).

At this time C Section had a new officer, we were sorry to lose "Jimmy" Revill: he wasn't sorry to lose us, I'm sure. One day while on a route march, the new officer lost his section, that is to say he was lost in the crisscross of lanes. As he was leading the section, we were all lost. Everyone was thinking that it was a longer route than usual, feeling a little hungry and footsore. The singing became less spirited and someone muttered, "I bet we're lost." We were, though not told officially of course. The singing stopped altogether as we realised that we might be a long way from tea and that the medical orderlies would be off duty by the time we reached the site, if we reached the site. After a route march anyone who needed foot medication reported to the MI room.

The landscape was flat and looked the same in any direction without landmarks, the farms dotted here and there were low, single-storey buildings in the Scottish style. It was a cloudy grey day known as State C on the Command Post, so without sun our leader didn't know which direction he was leading us. We did make it, somewhat later than was usual, and our hut's inmates speculated as to whether the Officers' Mess would find out why C section were on such a long route march. Judging by the talk and laughter in the dining hall at teatime there was no doubt that the incident would filter through to the Officers' Mess via the Sergeants' Mess.

The next time we paraded for a route march, instead of hearing the order "Section will move to the left in threes, left wheel" as we reached the gate, the command was given for us to wheel to the right, large grins on the faces of us all. Thinking that we would be marching along the main road and had more chance of boosting the public's morale, we were surprised when, a little way along the road towards Edinburgh and the Forth Bridge, we heard the Sergeant's. voice bellowing "Section will move to the left in threes, left wheel." Obeying the command we found ourselves in a narrow winding lane leading downwards towards the water which, though visible, turned out to be three miles away. Arriving at the bottom the section was halted and told to "Fall Out." Told to re-assemble at a certain time, we could hardly believe our good fortune. Not the usual ten minutes' break but three-quarters of an hour to sit on the grass and look at the water from the tiny harbour. The road ended there; Blackness had a ruined castle, an hotel and a few cottages.

As it was afternoon the hotel wasn't open, even had anyone been allowed to enter, which I doubt. Our lot headed for the ruins and the grass scattered with boulders which had fallen from the walls. We explored, climbed, ran, shouted down dungeons, or what we thought were dungeons, like children let out of school. The unexpected freedom had gone to our heads. Hatless, we revelled in the sunshine and I lost my cap badge. I hoped it wouldn't be noticed but it was, so I was in trouble for going hatless. I couldn't expect the Sergeant to believe that the badge could fall out of the cap while it was on my head.

Later, on an evening pass, a group of us walked down to Blackness to find out if the hotel served food. A meal could be booked in advance; there was no choice of menu though, just whatever they could rustle up, eggs mainly as I remember. It was pleasant to have supper there, you couldn't call it dinner. It was served in a sitting room which had a huge fire and an enormous settee which you sank in to. I went there for supper several times with a male escort and the two of us often were the sole occupants. There was a small bar and an even smaller cocktail lounge, but for us the comfort and privacy was all we needed. Unless with a male escort the ATS didn't think it was worth walking three miles there and back for, that was the only way to get there (no bus).

I don't know how we earned the reputation of being a noisy hut, maybe being near the Battery Office had something to do with it. Avalon, a corporal said, our hut should be named as it was the exact opposite to earthly paradise. The next day, a gunner who obviously agreed made a nameplate bearing the name "Avalon Hut 10" and fastened it beside the door. We were quite tickled, but fully expected to be ordered to remove it by the powers that be; however, there it stayed and sadly when we moved to another site, no one thought to take it with us. About the same time a bombardier wrote a few verses and stuck them up in the NAAFI.

Quite an assortment of literature ended up on the NAAFI walls at Merrilees. Statements like "Britain blancos while Russia bleeds", "Never have so many waited so long for so little", "Yanks are overpaid, over-sexed and over here". The NAAFI staff were tolerant, but then they never came the other side of the counter. The gunners cleaned the canteen as part of their duties. The words relating to our hut were as follows:

> There's a wooden hut called Avalon
> with the sign of number ten
> where a gang of beauties hang out
> and they never go with men.
>
> The one in charge is Corporal Crisp
> We call her Chips for short
> she says the men around the camp
> are really not her sort.
>
> There's Vera Podge and Mary
> and Margaret Urquhart too

> *and Dorothy Nan and Edna*
> *with Billie makes the crew.*
>
> *Now Podge is a spotter*
> *and so is Billie Hague*
> *while Chippy works the Plotter*
> *through why is rather vague.*
>
> *They get 24 hrs. together*
> *and paint Queensferry red*
> *while Podge stays with her Sergeant*
> *when she should be tucked in bed.*
>
> *The nose that often comes from ten*
> *tells you that Spitfire's there*
> *and sometimes Mary cracks a joke*
> *that makes you want to swear.*
>
> *They're really quite a happy crowd*
> *and get on well together*
> *but they like me, will all be glad*
> *when we leave this land of heather.*
> Bdr. Nobby Clark 1943

The hut corporal wrote it in my autograph book afterwards. On one heated occasion, someone called me Spitfire and the name stuck. If it really applied then I must have changed a lot since donning khaki uniform.

Merrilees was further from civilisation than F site had been; though buses did run between Boness and Edinburgh, the service was sparse. Distances too were lengthy, Edinburgh was the longest journey. Boness was not convenient for an evening pass, buses ran at awkward times and it was in the opposite direction from South Queensferry, about an equal distance away. South Queensferry suited the ATS for an evening pass yet was still far enough away to mean a two-hour walk if you were so unfortunate as to miss the last bus. Oh how we moaned about missing the last waltz every time, but I only remember walking back the long road once.

The great attraction was the naval base Port Edgar; the whole area was full of the Royal Navy and Royal Marines. Many ships lay in the Firth of Forth, all shapes and sizes from Battleships to Motor Torpedo Boats (MTBs) being repaired, refitted or assembling in convoy to escort ships of the Merchant Navy in their hazardous task of trying to bring essential supplies to Britain.

The village consisted of one main street running alongside the water. There was a cinema, a post office, two cafes, a fish and chip shop and Roseberry Hall where we danced. Several pubs of course, but they didn't rate highly on our list of priorities. Regular dances were held at the naval base and film shows too, which uniformed personnel could attend, so with all that entertainment who needed pubs? Our association with the boys in navy blue was long and enjoyable. Ships came into the Forth and went out again into more dangerous waters. Some stayed longer than others, but they all went away eventually.

Edinburgh was a costly excursion; we couldn't afford to go as often as we wished. Sometimes we would go to Boness for the afternoon on a 24-hr leave. It boasted a cinema, a service canteen and a few shops. The Masonic Hall sometimes held dances in a beautiful panelled room. No YWCA hostel, so it meant going back to camp – cheaper of course. We saved up for trips to Edinburgh.

One night Stevenson and I were on 24 hours together in Boness. We had been to the cinema in the afternoon and to a dance in the evening when the inevitable happened, we missed the bus back. There was nothing for it but to set off on shanks's pony. Although our legs and feet were nearly the fittest in the Battery and were still capable of dancing the rest of the night away if required, the long dark walk was a gloomy prospect. However, not altogether cheerful but singing as soon as we had left the houses and pavements, we decided that if we sang marching songs and pretended to be on a route march, we'd get along quicker. There was little hope of a lift, nothing much was ever on the roads at night owing to petrol rationing, but after a while we stopped singing to listen, in the hope that a military vehicle might be abroad. It was a murky night; if there had been any stars we'd have wished on a star.

After some miles, silent by now except for our marching feet, something on wheels glided to a stop beside us and a voice was heard. "Ye can hae a lift if ye're no feared, I'm driving a hearse!" Thankfully we climbed in to find it unoccupied in the back, the driver had a companion sitting beside him. We didn't ask why the hearse happened to be on the road at the particular time, it was wiser not to ask questions. Naturally, no one believed us when we told them the next day. When they did accept, somewhat dubiously, our account of the inopportune ride, the older ones lectured us on the possible dangers we may have faced.

Another item for discussion round the hut fire centred on the many possible reasons why the vehicle was on that road that night. All sorts of improbable suggestions were put forward resulting in hilarious peals of laughter. The simple answer would be that someone had misused the vehicle to go on a quite innocent errand and because of the petrol rationing and restrictions war had brought, thought justifiable. Stevenson and I said we would accept a lift on a muck cart sooner than face that walk again, or in the hearse if it was available. Not all of those sitting round the fire agreed with us about the latter. It was a bit weird we admitted, but preferable to foot-slogging in the dark. After listening to all our conclusions and hilarity, Hunt the ex-Nanny said seriously, "I don't suppose either of you two irresponsible girls considered that you might have been raped?"

"What could be worse than being raped in a hearse?" said Urquhart and off we all went again into hoots.

"Be serious," said Hunt, "suppose the two men had raped you then dumped you in a ditch; even if they didn't murder you first, imagine having to report the facts. No one would be able to trace the men and I don't suppose you noticed the number of the hearse did you? Or, ... " she said ponderously when the screeches of mirth had died down "did you stop to consider they might be German spies?"

"Not with an accent like that," said Stevenson. "Mind you, Thomson deciphered his words. I thought he was foreign, but I know German when I hear it, even if I don't understand it."

One day four of us from Avalon were in Boness on our way to the cinema matinee and called in a shop first to see if there was anything not on ration that we could buy to take with us. Podge was our best scrounger, she had a nose for it – perhaps that is too harsh a word, charm would be more accurate. That girl could charm the birds from the trees, usually in her own interests but sometimes we would benefit. Men had no chance if she turned her innocent big blue eyes in their direction. Her own sex too, us included, found themselves doing things and going places they hadn't really intended going. The lady in the shop was a walkover for Podge but in all fairness to that lady, she was such a kind and generous person herself as it turned out, that we'd have done quite as well without Podge.

It must have involved a lot of extra work especially for the little shopkeepers during rationing and if they did get a little extra for whatever reason, the Boness lady certainly shared her rations with others, namely us. She lived with her sixteen-year-old daughter, Christine, above the shop, who she told us couldn't wait to be old enough to join one of the services. Whatever we acquired from the shop I don't remember, but it was something to eat and we bought other off-ration commodities like toothpaste and writing paper. Non-rationed goods were often hard to come by.

The upshot of our profitable visit was that we enjoyed much hospitality in that home and stayed overnight on 24 hours many times. We took Christine with us to the cinema and dances and regaled them both with our stories of incidents which broke the pattern of our days. Nothing of military significance passed our lips naturally, but things like when one morning half a dozen of us entered the ablutions to get a shock, literally.

As taps were turned on shouts of fright and screams were heard, all the metal was live. Half naked, we ran outside to warn the others not to enter. We were making such a din that no one could understand what was wrong at first. It was a crazy scene that morning, six near hysterical females and others looking bewildered. Dressed in greatcoats over pyjamas or less, feet shod in unlaced boots, carrying towels and toothbrushes, thinking there were parachutists in the ablutions to cause the commotion. There had been a rumour flying round that one had been seen in the area.

We were supposed to be fully clad when out of doors but it seemed to the ATS a complete waste of time to get dressed only to undress again to wash. Some took their clothes down with them but there was no place to hang them except over the water pipes where they were likely to get wet. Each day, therefore, it meant a manoeuvre, avoiding the square and dodging round huts, peering round corners like Chad to avoid being seen by an NCO on the long trek to water.

Later on that day we were allowed to use the men's ablutions, but for the first half of the day the ATS remained unwashed. Whatever happened in the army, parades took place at the usual times. The reason why the taps gave off electric shocks was never explained, but all was made safe by the REME squad; mutters were heard about sabotage though.

Christine thought our uniforms smart, but as she learned more about our lives on a gunsite she told us that the WRNS were billeted in large houses in the area and therefore life would not be so spartan. The WRNS hats were more flattering anyway, she added. Obviously Christine was not blessed with an adventurous spirit for which her mother was thankful and we assured her optimistically that the war would be over before Christine was of age to join anything.

Some time after settling in at Merrilees, our hut acquired a gramophone and a few records. We clubbed together and bought more as our meagre funds would allow. Equal work did not mean equal pay; the ATS received two thirds of a soldiers basic pay. One night after Lights Out, the gramophone was still playing, needless to say the hut corporal wasn't in residence at the time, she was either on leave or away on a course. Everyone was in bed except me, sitting huddled over the last embers and playing requests. Nelson Eddy was singing "Wanting You" from the show *New Moon*; it was my favourite. Suddenly there was a loud banging on the door and an angry male voice shouted "I'll be wanting you in the Orderly Room in the morning: shut that bloody noise off!" – the unmistakable tones of Lieutenant "Dickie" Dunt the Orderly Officer.

There was a hushed silence as I snatched off the needle, we

listened to his footsteps going away along the frosty path then each bed shook as the restrained laughter exploded, I was the only one not laughing. Trouble again and the prospect of those awful cookhouse tins. The next morning fully expecting to be put on a charge or at the very least told to report for extra duties after tea, I awaited my fate. Nothing happened and I kept wondering when I'd be sent for. After dinner and the main parade I began to relax, it seemed I had been reprieved. That song was spoilt for me for ever though, because whenever it was played the others in the hut would all sing "I'll be wanting you in the Orderly Room" and the romantic mood was lost while everyone had a fit of giggles again.

Another activity round the fire was mending, necessary at least monthly for we had a kit inspection every month – kit had all to be laid out on beds. We hated these evenings, I don't suppose the ATS officer relished them either. She and the Orderly Sergeant would go the rounds of all the ATS huts, they checked for buttons on shirts and darns in socks. Most of us had to learn how to darn socks and darn them neatly for our own benefit, so when kit inspection was due there would be a darning session round the fire. Our grey woollen socks were exactly the same issue as the men's.

The kit had to be laid out in a certain way. With so many items to place neatly on a narrow bed, it seemed impossible. We had learned of course to do this at Arborfield and the hut corporal had drawn a plan. Woe betide anyone who had a button missing or shoes without hobnails. Immediately kit inspection was over, Hague being the one with the scout knife, had to remove them all. She had in the beginning, rashly volunteered to do this. They had to be hammered in again before the next kit inspection so we always had to keep in a supply. It was bad enough having to wear heavy clumpy shoes in the first place, but with hobnails in, two of us walking sounded like a squad at least. I think the hobnail order only applied to Ack Ack.

Captain Funnell, our site CO, formed a mixed Hockey team. He was one of the officers who regarded the ATS as gunners in every sense, so he had the wholehearted loyalty and respect of every girl on site. Being much older than any of us, he was a kind of Father figure, though I don't suppose he would have been flattered to know that. Other officers had mixed feelings about girls and it showed, not openly but in various ways. One important thing which I learned at Durham and one I never forgot – that when saluting an officer, to remember that it was the King's Commission uniform you were saluting and not the person wearing it.

Sometimes the junior officers were moved from one half of the Battery to the other. One of these was 2nd Lieutenant. Lacy – Snaky Lacy we called him. The ATS were pleased to see him go and didn't hide the fact. It's hard to explain as no one had a specific reason for disliking him, it was his manner towards us. The senior officers and NCOs stayed put and strangely enough the ones who bawled and shouted at us, if for a good reason, we respected. In other words, if we were treated as RA gunners, which we were, we reacted accordingly.

Because hockey was the only thing in school sport I was any good at, I was in the team along with Hague and Odgers. The CO arranged matches with other service teams, mainly army and navy, and we played home and away matches within the area. I looked forward to these weekly games, especially the away ones – we always stayed out for tea. When we played against a naval team at Boness one Sunday the girls went to the WRNS quarters for tea, it was revelation to us. Compared to ours their billets were luxurious, in a large private house, still furnished. We had tea in a large room furnished with a huge settee and lots of deep armchairs. Before a crackling fire we scoffed an old-fashioned afternoon tea, sandwiches, scones, tea, bread and cakes.

Hague went back to camp afterwards and Odgers and I, because we were on a 24-hr leave, were invited by the WRNS to go to a dance with them and stay the night. We jumped at the offer, it mattered not a jot that we had to doss down in their comfy sitting room.

Cupid's Arrows

Letters ran like a jewelled thread through our days and were the link between us and those from whom we were parted. From home, from the high seas and from battlefields covering nearly half the world the letters came. War went on far longer than anyone predicted. Not all the letters bore good news, far from it. Many brought tears and heartache as husbands, brothers, fathers, boyfriends, cousins and uncles were reported missing, taken prisoner, wounded or killed.

Mail from overseas was always censored and eventually outgoing mail from military sources came under censorship too. We were quite used to writing letters leaving out any reference to our lives inside the camp, the subject of weather was also taboo. It was quite another thing, however, to write endearments knowing that someone else would be reading them. The backs of envelopes would make interesting reading for the Post orderly, as scrawled on them would be an assortment of codes. The most common was SWALK which means Sealed with a loving kiss. Others were FAAD – Forever and a day: WMA – We'll meet again: LYFE Love you for ever: MLA – My love always, and lots more. The next one seems to beg a question ITALY – I trust and love you.

Sometimes the censor used blue pencil, but more often than not he would use scissors. One day a girl received the remains of such a letter. It was in ribbons with strips cut out from most of it, the writer had used both sides of the paper which made matters worse. The poor recipient passed it round to see if anyone could decipher anything more than she had managed –

only the romantic beginning and end were intact. She saw the funny side of it and later stuck it up in the NAAFI so that people queuing at the counter could test their wits or have a guess what the writer had written. For a week or two it caused laughter as the witty ones read between the lines with words of their own.

A band was formed and dances on Sunday evenings became a regular feature. We were allowed to invite other service personnel, but no civilians were allowed on site. Hague played the accordion, Lieutenant. Emerson (he of the dust) the fiddle, another officer the double bass, Bdrs Wilson and Clark the drums. The pianists varied – whoever reached the piano first, I think.

We still had the odd concert from either local or army sources, but after the formation of the band we decided to have another go at producing our own. Rehearsals were funnier than the actual concert. We didn't attempt anything like a play with long parts to learn. As it was, the instigators had a hard enough task enlisting enough artistes to make the project worthwhile. Once rehearsals had begun, the cast threw themselves into it with gusto. I could only persuade two from Avalon to take part, Podge and Hague.

Not having access to costumes or anyone's attic, it was a case of making do with army clothing or whatever we could beg. Towels and sheets (only recently issued to ATS), cookhouse tins, storm lanterns and the only non-issue lady's nightie on site. Apart from musical items the concert was a series of short sketches intermingled with songs by a group of ATS and some community singing, Bdr. Wilson was compere. We didn't choose the sketches then look for props, it was a case of "What have we got?" and then write something round the props. Not really exciting enough to stage an extravaganza with, but we did our best and enjoyed it all even if we couldn't be sure that the audience did.

During the summer the CO decided to hold a Sports Day on site and ordered a sunny day for the event. The day dawned hot and sunny and the war seemed far away. Everyone in shorts and shirts, hatless and without ties, bare legs wearing canvas shoes; freedom indeed – it felt wonderful. I didn't win any races though I entered them all except the water pole. This was a large tank full of water and a pole placed above it horizontally. Two contestants sat on this and tried to knock each other off with sandbags which had some of the sand taken out. You needed to be a swimmer if you fell into the tank. Stevenson was the only one in our hut to win an event: with a set chin she knocked all her opponents into the water. I don't remember which section won the most points and it didn't matter for it was a great day, thoroughly enjoyed by all except a few unfortunate people. Two spotters, the four on guard, two Command Post telephonists, a clerk in Battery Office and the one casualty of the day, A D section Height-finder operator who fell and broke a leg.

That summer too we witnessed a tragedy. A small plane carrying an army officer hit some wires near our site and came down in flames. He and the pilot were dead by the time anyone reached the scene.

Russia being one of our allies, much sympathy was felt for them and several gunners, male and female, could enliven an argument or discussion by showing themselves to be sympathetic to the Communist cause. A few dull evenings could thus be livened up by such a topic. One day on parade we were being detailed for extra duties, like painting stones, edging the paths and cutting grass with shears and scissors – lawn mowers were not on the army list of essential equipment. A lick of paint here, more spit and polish there, tea buckets like mirrors, all the fire buckets washed and every lurking cigarette end removed. Colonel Hogben (Algy) the CO of the Regiments was due to pay us a visit.

The assembled gunners were standing at ease listening to the Orderly Sergeant when a male voice from within the ranks muttered "Britain blancos while Russia bleeds."

A roar from the Sergeant, "One pace forward that man."

No one moved: the Sergeant roared again, "That was an order, the whole lot of you will be on a charge if the order is not obeyed!" Three male gunners stepped forward one pace, a second later the whole parade did likewise. There was a few seconds silence then another roar. "Parade, parade, 'shun, dismiss." We all went off to our allotted tasks in silence and that was the end of that.

The Colonel's visit over, life went on much as before. Then one day the ATS were given a lesson in map reading (Ordnance Survey). After one session in the lecture hut we were then sent out in groups armed with a map and told not to get lost. After only one short lesson, to half of the girls it was still as clear as mud. The rest of us couldn't see the point of learning map reading unless, as one girl put it, the officers knew something which they weren't telling us!

We pondered this for a while, invasion on our minds again, then as usual someone said something silly: laughter and wild speculations as to the reason for this new venture. In all other army aspects we had striven to excel; it was strange, therefore, that this latest skill was not being taken seriously by any of us.

Although everyone arrived back from the first excursion safely, it was more by good luck than management and even though the exercise continued, we didn't derive the benefit from it that we should have. Fortunately, we were never put through a test on the subject, we would all have failed I'm sure. Maybe someone in the Officers' Mess thought we ought to be trained in map reading in case we ever got lost on a route march again. Whatever the reason, neither the officers or the Sergeants appeared to be enthusiastic about it. The colder weather had arrived and though the trees looked beautiful in their autumn colours and we enjoyed the forays into the countryside, one and all were thankful when Battery Orders ceased to print Map Reading as a weekly event.

Our dances were held alternate Sundays, the band performing for the other half of the Battery the other Sunday. One evening just after the band had got into its stride, (it took a little while sometimes to get into strict tempo, there was no time for band rehearsal, they just played each Sunday like heroes enduring the grumbles from the experts about the beat being wrong or the waltz too fast), there came through the door a group of new faces, all male. They received a warm welcome, naturally; not many of our own males were dancers and there were never enough visitors – I don't think the refreshments exactly tempted many.

The quick-thinking band leader announced a Ladies' Choice waltz and every newcomer was on the floor at the first bar of

I'll be with you in apple blossom time. We found out that the newcomers were part of a very small group of Royal Engineers camped somewhere in a wood on the banks of the Forth halfway between our gunsite and South Queensferry. Having no canteen facilities they were to use our NAAFI so we got to know them all quite well. Not all of them could dance when they arrived, but the ATS took care of that and in a few weeks, although not as good as Victor Sylvester, they were proficient enough not to cripple their partners. Even though we suspected that one or two might have been married, we enjoyed the company of the REs at our dances and sometimes in the NAAFI.

We didn't know what they were engaged in there in the wood, they didn't tell us and we knew better than to ask. It wasn't until months after the war had ended, that I discovered why that small contingent of soldiers had been camped so well-hidden in a wood. They worked for Ordnance Survey in civilian life and it was their duty to be taken by submarine to the French coast to collect soil, beach and rock samples. Then to analyse and make maps in preparation for the D-day landings along the French beaches. They entered the water in the Firth of Forth and returned the same way. No mail was delivered there, one of them collected it from a post office. Ours was the only NAAFI they used, their officer was a guest in our Officers' Mess. Only a few knew of their existence and two months later they were gone. They landed on that French beach again on D-day plus two.

During the time they were with us, friendships were made between the ATS and the Royal Engineers so even more letters were written and received in our mail bag. After the REs had gone to "Somewhere in England" (that was their address – included was name, rank, number, another code number and Royal Engineers), I received letters from one of them and of course wrote in reply. His name was Bob and he was from Yorkshire where they play good cricket he told me. He had been one of the non-dancers before reaching our site, but when he left he was passable due to the joint efforts of Cpl. Loveridge who took the ATS for PT, Stevenson, Urquhart and me. Bob always asked me for the last waltz and '*La Mere*", the tune often played by our band for the last waltz, will always remind me of him and those other RE soldiers who were our guests.

Christmas '43 came and went; the fighting overseas was bitter and costly in human life, at sea the story was the same. Letters told us more than the newspapers did of the misery of war and the effect it was having on the lives of ordinary people, embroiled through no fault of their own in the horror of war caused by greed for power by some and lack of foresight by others. We didn't have a "best-dressed hut competition", neither did we decorate our hut that Christmas.

The January gales roared round Avalon finding their way through every nook and cranny and we huddled round our fire, supplemented by firewood from our copse and anything else we found burnable. All of us were duty bound to keep eyes skinned when out of camp for fallen branches on the lanes.

My 21st birthday was in January and my mother, as well as sending a cake and other presents, sent money for a bottle of whatever I could get for the others to toast me on reaching adulthood! The hotel in Blackness, where I had spent several evenings with Bob, had promised to let me have a bottle of port wine to celebrate my birthday. On an evening pass previous to the birthday I was to collect it. Down the long dark lane Stevenson and I went, she grumbling that we could have been in Queensferry instead of taking all night to fetch a bottle of port which she didn't like anyway. She said cheerful things like, they probably wouldn't have it when we got there, she was sure it was going to rain and that it wouldn't be very nice drinking wine from enamel mugs. I told her airily that I was going to borrow wine glasses from the Officers' Mess. That shut her up for a few minutes and while she was deciding whether I was kidding or not we reached the hotel, collected the precious bottle (well-wrapped) and we both plodded back up the hill to Merrilees.

The birthday of course was just like any other day, the morning NAAFI break when the mail was given out was no more looked forward to than every other day. In the evening I cut the cake, un-iced with apologies from Mum, and we drank the port from enamel mugs except Stevenson of course. I was grown up and should have had the key of the door except that there was no key. There were no locks on any door but the Ammunition Store, Kit Store and the Cookhouse.

The Battleship HMS Royal Sovereign was lying at anchor in the Firth of Forth having recently returned from America where it had undergone a refit. The British crew were awaiting the arrival of a Russian crew, for the Battleship was being handed over to the Russian Navy. One Sunday the Orderly Sergeant asked for volunteers from those ATS starting a 24-hr leave to accept an invitation from the Royal Sovereign to board the Battleship, have a guided tour round it and take tea with the crew. Some of the girls in true army tradition hesitated – "never volunteer for anything" in their minds vying with "what shall I miss if I don't volunteer?" – but Urquhart, Odgers, Stevenson and I, in that order, accepted at once.

I wasn't as thrilled as the others about the forthcoming afternoon treat for I had a problem. Up to that moment I had managed to hide the fact that I was terrified of being on water. I liked to be beside water, walking, sitting or just looking at it, but only unwillingly would I venture upon it. The times the Hockey team crossed the ferry when playing at Rossyth or Dunfermline were purgatory for me. The ferryboat was bigger than the small launch that would transport us from the quay out into the middle of the Forth; I didn't think I could face it, not even for the British Navy. I couldn't think of a plausible excuse either, our fortnightly dance was being held in the evening. If I pleaded sudden illness I could hardly make a quick recovery to attend that. I just hoped that I wouldn't disgrace the Royal Artillery or the ATS by having to be dragged on board at the water's edge.

I certainly didn't want anyone to know about my phobia, I hated being made fun of but had learned to pretend that I could take it. Some things I was more sensitive about than others and I never really came to terms with the fact that, living in such a close environment, our lives were open books to those with whom we shared the hut. The lesser of two evils then was to act, to show excitement on actually being invited on board a British Battleship which had been in action; oh how I wished she had been in dry dock. As we cleaned buttons, shoes and cap badges, my terror mounted. The dreaded hour approached and I was still searching for a way out as, with the group of girls, I stepped smartly down the lane.

The small naval launch awaiting us tossed in the waves. Out of vanity none of us were wearing greatcoats and the January wind was making us regret the fact. Of all the things I was called upon during my war service to attempt, boarding that bobbing craft with a frozen smile on my face was one of the most difficult. The worst was yet to come, I had to climb out of the launch and up a rope ladder to the deck which towered above me. Battleships may look massive when viewed from a distance, but from below at water level that one looked gigantic. I wasn't the first one on the rope and I wasn't the last either, that was only because I was manhandled on to the first rung by a hefty sailor. Show a leg he said, I couldn't do anything else but show a lot of leg, nor could the other girls, ATS skirts weren't meant for mountaineering up the sides of His Majesty's Battleships.

Once safely on board we were welcomed and, in groups, escorted on a ship's tour which was impressive; we were all interested in the guns, naturally. The sailors showed surprise until we enlightened them to the fact that we were gunners and not just ordinary ATS. I don't think they all believed us though, judging by the looks on their faces and some of their remarks. It would be my misfortune to be in a group with one of these Doubting Thomases, just as I was thinking that I'd invite him to our dance and hoped he could dance, he asked if any of us would care to climb up to the crows nest; that put me off him. The six of us gazed upwards then looked at each other, no one seemed enthusiastic and the wind was making howling noises. We all had cap bands under our chins in case we lost our caps and would have been quite happy for the tour to end there. We'd seen the crows nest, that was enough. With a wicked gleam in his eye he dared us to climb up. There was no way out of that, the honour of the Battery was at stake and of all ATS serving in Ack Ack. I've never been keen on heights and would have declined politely had I found the courage, coward that I was.

Never let it be said that 536 refused a challenge and up we went. I knew I shouldn't have set out on that mad adventure, I told myself as I gripped the cold metal. Closing my eyes when I reached the top, not daring to look at that wide expanse of water, I concentrated all my thoughts on remembering how to get down again. Suppose one of us had been blown off or fainted or something we asked each other afterwards, who would have been blamed? Probably us for being so foolhardy as to go up. More cause for merriment in the hut when we returned to tell of our afternoon on board ship and suggestions for newspaper headlines if one or more of us had not survived the crows nest. Thankfully, we all did without disgracing ourselves, though on reaching the deck I found it difficult to walk as my legs seemed to have been replaced by rubber ones. I pretended that the wind was too strong for me: pretending had become a habit.

Never was a cup of tea more welcome than the one waiting for us in the Mess. The tea spread before us was certainly better than the one they would be having on the gunsite. American goodies in tins (or cans in American terms), delicious peaches, cream, salmon and ham were there in plenty – we ate our fill. One thing only prevented me from enjoying that meal one hundred per cent and that was the thought of the journey back to dry land. It wasn't any better on the way back than the way out, except that it was the way back and the ordeal was nearly over. I had rubber legs again when I staggered out of the launch and was sure I'd never be able to dance for weeks. That day may not be in the Royal Navy's book of records, but it was certainly in mine.

All the ATS had invited their hosts to the dance, it appeared, so there was a good sprinkling of navy blue among the khaki uniforms that night and when I found myself on the dance floor with one in navy blue to the strains of a dreamy waltz, my legs were back to normal.

Cupid had been aboard The Royal Sovereign that day and Urquhart had been pierced by one of his darts. She had eyes for no other and from then on her evening leaves were spent with her Prince Charming. In vain Stevenson and I tried to coax her to go dancing with us as usual and not spend all her free time with her sailor boy. We told her that sailors were supposed to have a wife in every port and that he'd be going away any day when the Russian sailors arrived, but she was in love and starry-eyed. We had a whirlwind romance on our hands and were not sure of its outcome.

Defending The Bridge

Exactly two weeks later, Urquhart was due for leave and, a few days beforehand, informed us that she was going to meet Geoffrey's parents; it was serious then on both sides. After spending a week with her own parents first, Urquhart arranged to meet her sailor *en route* to London at Newcastle-on-Tyne station. They met as thousands of other couples met and parted on railway platforms in wartime, Geoffrey proposed and Margaret Urquhart accepted.

Joyously, they boarded the London bound train and when Urquhart discovered that her fiancé had omitted to tell his parents about her, she was just a shade worried. Not for long though, it had all happened so quickly and she was still up in the clouds, nothing could go wrong, everything was wonderful. Urquhart of course had told her parents about Geoffrey on account of only spending part of her leave with them, but they hadn't met him.

To say that the London parents were taken by surprise was putting it mildly, but they welcomed the Scottish girl and the newly engaged couple spent a happy week with them. It was Urquhart's first visit to London and in spite of being a city girl she was impressed. After all there is no other city quite like London, even scarred by bomb damage, with sandbags and blackouts, there was a special feeling about it. Surrounded by all its history, some of the famous buildings battered, its citizens too, there was still an undercurrent of determination about it. Though the enemy was sure that if London were brought to her knees, then the rest of the country would be a walkover. The air raids became intensified again that February.

Urquhart returned from leave ecstatic with happiness: she glowed and we were all glad for her, what else could we be! One or two of us in Avalon had reservations though, I for one. It all seemed too sudden, they didn't really know one another. With our usual candour and habit of discussing the affairs of all within our hut, we said this to Urquhart, but it fell on deaf ears. The rest, caught up in the excitement of the romance, disagreed with the cautious ones and pointed out that it was happening all the time.

A week or two later our minds were filled with something else. We were to move over to the other site, HQ would remain there and C and D Sections would therefore be HQ site. We wondered whether it would make much difference to our lives, there would be more NCOs and officers about, an RSM for one thing who had a reputation, the usual army one. It didn't really affect us, everyone was as smart and well drilled in everything as they could possibly be, plus the fact that we knew all eyes would be on us. If a comparison was being made then C and D would show them; we didn't need to be told by now, it was instinctive.

The weeks went by till one day Urquhart announced that the Russian crew had arrived and the crew of The Royal Sovereign had received postings to join another ship at Chatham and that Geoffrey wanted them to be married before the posting, which set us all in a flurry. At that time only 24 hours' posting up of banns was required for a marriage to take place and the bridegroom lost no time in arranging things.

Urquhart's parents were not in favour of the rush, but the couple went ahead without delay. They were to marry in the Registry Office in South Queensferry it was decided, and Geoffrey turned up at the gate one day requesting that his bride be allowed out to sign some documents for the ceremony to take place on the Friday, four days later. This was refused: Urquhart was on duty but she was determined to go out, pass or no pass. We advised her not to seek trouble, as did the Orderly Sergeant, there would be another way we told her. To no avail, she went to the hut and started to change from battledress into service dress, a few of us pleading with her to be sensible. When was a maiden in love ever sensible? The upshot was that she was escorted everywhere she went on site until bedtime and verbal messages were carried by a Cpl between the couple. Geoffrey was waiting in the guardroom while all this was going on. He went back to the Registrar, explained the situation and collected the papers to be signed and brought them back to the site where Urquhart signed them.

On Friday 15th April 1944, on a 24-hr pass, Margaret married Geoffrey with Mary Stevenson and Charlie, a fellow crew member of Geoffrey's, as witnesses. As a special dispensation, the Military Police allowed the four to embark on the ferry and to cross to North Queensferry for the wedding breakfast and the couple spent one night's honeymoon at an hotel.

Then it was back to duty for Urquhart or rather Creighton. It was ages before we got used to calling her by her new name. Eleven weeks from the visit to the battleship lying in the Forth we now had a married woman in our midst. To say that it didn't make any difference between us would be untrue, for one thing it wasn't quite the same when we went dancing. Although Creighton still loved dancing, she didn't look forward to dancing with anyone else but her husband and we found ourselves going to the cinema more often if we were all three on a pass together. It was only days of course before the couple were parted and the ship sailed away down to the open sea and Russia.

Another whirlwind courtship set everyone in a mood for romance, and one or two being carried on by letter had flourished, when one day I entered our hut to find a girl from D Section, one half of the whirlwind, standing on a kit box arrayed in a beautiful white wedding dress. It was borrowed and as no one in her own hut was any good with a needle, she had come to us for help. Stevenson and Amy were down on their knees pinning up the hem from which, somewhat incongruously, peeped a pair of feet shod in army boots. There was an air of spring, girls were singing at their cookhouse chores of *Flowers that Bloom Tra La* and *The Parson's Waiting For Me and My Girl*.

A day or so after the bride's fitting, she was sobbing to Stevenson and I in a quiet corner of a cafe in Queensferry after throwing her engagement ring across the table. It fell on to the floor and Stevenson quietly retrieved it and slipped it into her pocket while we waited for the sobs to cease. There is nothing you can do except be there close to the one who is suffering until she wants to talk it through, and this we did with our own tears welling up. Fortunately, the cafe was empty apart from us that afternoon. The brokenhearted girl told us, when she was able, that she had received a letter from her fiancé telling her that he had just married someone else. Of all the sad and miserable ending to engagements, that was the most cruel I knew of.

The end of the Forth Bridge actually was in Dalmeny, a village high up, looking down on the water which was a twenty-five-minute walk away, longer on the way back. If catching a bus it could be done in less time. There was a short cut, two in fact, both precarious in the dark. One was a steep flight of steps cut into the hill right underneath the bridge itself, so you ended up opposite the ferry. The other one went off the road through some allotments, zig-zagging between houses perched on the hillside, terminating at the end of an entry between the cinema and Roseberry Hall.

Dalmeny had a small station and almost every train was stopped before crossing the bridge. The reason for this wasn't divulged, but one reason could be heard. The wheels of the engines were tapped and examined, the metallic clunking became a familiar sound, but what was significant to us was that it meant coal, lovely coal. From arriving at Dalmeny site we received a regular supply of coal courtesy of LNER, unofficially that was. Our hut was adjacent to the track where the wheel-tapping was done and engine drivers threw lumps of coal down beside the hedge. Any tapping activity was the signal for anyone from our hut not on manning duty to go as quickly as possible, without being spotted by an NCO, to the scene of the operation. She would creep through a convenient gap in the hedge and drag the coal through, hide it in the ditch at the back of the hut and return to her duties. Goodness knows how long that had been practised, but we considered ourselves lucky to be nearest to the supply and were grateful to whoever had instigated the exercise. As we had the most devious ones in our lot, we acquired more loot and had the hottest fires on the site.

One night when a gale was blowing, the pipe leading from the stove top to the wooden roof glowed red and we were all a little worried that any minute the hut would go up in flames. The next morning when it was cool, flakes of metal fell off the pipe: we took more care in future watching anxiously for a hole to appear. We would never have been able to give a suitable explanation with the meagre ration of coke issued, as to how a hole had burnt through a chimney pipe. We also had the most soot and frequently two of us, always Hague and either Stevenson, Odgers or I, would shin up on the roof to remove as much of it as we could without proper equipment.

One afternoon word got round that the ATS huts were to have a surprise inspection: these spot checks happened from time to time, luckily someone always found out. Then whoever could leave whatever they were doing to scamper off unseen, would whizz into their own hut, remove whatever was lying about that shouldn't be, as quickly as possible, hoping to do this before Orderly Officer and Orderly Sergeant arrived. The huts and folded blankets had to remain immaculate all day till gunners were dismissed from duties prior to tea parade. We were allowed to enter huts during the dinner break, but had to make sure that there wasn't a towel spread out to dry or a book thrown on a bed (there inevitably was, hence the irregular inspections).

That particular day, whoever had been delegated to light the fire had placed a large lump of coal in the hearth ready for breaking up. Apart from the fact it shouldn't have been there in the first place, it was contraband. We would have a hard job explaining it away. The runner quickly lifted the lid of the nearest kit box and placed the coal on top of a newly laundered pile of white vests and panties.

The indignant owner of the kit box was livid when she discovered later that it had been used as a coal bin. She demanded to know who was responsible and her anger was such that those of us who knew the culprit kept quiet. Not one of us dare laugh until much later, it would have to be Hunt's box, she was extremely proud of her "whites" and washed all her own underwear, even her towels. Hunt was on manning duty so didn't know the identity of the culprit, for some reason she blamed me for I was on cookhouse fatigues and could have been the one, but I wasn't. It was Odgers, but no one ever told Hunt and she never forgave me for it.

Poor Hunt, she left us soon after that. She was released on medical grounds, the northern winters had caused spells of chronic bronchitis and for weeks she had difficulty breathing unless she slept sitting up. Stevenson and I saw her off at Waverly station in Edinburgh and after a few months convalescence, she took a post as Nanny once more, vowing never to leave the south again. Of course we all wrote to her and, as writing paper was in short supply like many other things, she made sure of receiving letters from us by sending me packets of stationery.

Whether it was Hunt being discharged that put the idea into Thomas's mind was not certain, but the Welsh girl in D Section kept on about headaches and she thought she ought to be discharged, until her hut mates were sick of hearing her going on about it. Like us they were loyal to each other and what they did or said in their own hut was kept between them.

Thomas's hut-mates one day decided to teach her a lesson, one of them filched an army release form from who knows where, filled it in and signed it with an indecipherable scrawl of a signature. In effect it said that she was being discharged in a month's time. She had been reporting sick with headaches and had told the others that the medical orderly had said if she stopped going to bed in a head full of metal curlers the headaches would stop, but Thomas didn't believe her. She said it was the noise of the guns when she was on manning duty that had left an echo in her head.

The form in a long brown envelope lay on her pile of blankets when they all trooped in the hut to get ready for tea. Their hut corporal told our hut corporal all this afterwards and she told the rest of us in confidence. We didn't hear it from any other source. The corporal wasn't in the know beforehand, someone told her just before they came down from the Command Post so she just had to wait and watch, a trifle anxious as to the outcome, not knowing what the victim's reaction might be.

Thomas opened the envelope while the others tried to act normally, a sudden hush would have warned her, all eyes were on her as she read the enclosure. She laid it down on top of the blankets without saying a word, undid her respirator, threw it down on the bed followed by her steel helmet, picked up the paper again and read it through. By that time there was a silence as they all wondered if it had been such a good joke after all. Thomas looked up. "They can't do this, I'm going to find the Orderly Sergeant," she said and started towards the door. At that, most of those in the hut burst into laughter except one or two who felt sorry then.

There was no doubt about it, the girl was upset and didn't really want her release, she was just a born moaner. She wept, whether from rage or relief was hard to tell, but she never mentioned release again. That same girl was a perpetual borrower and when her Welsh singsong was heard at our door "Can I come in?" we would shout in unison, "Whatever you want, we ain't got it." It didn't stop her coming again.

No one took offence; even if you felt a little hurt sometimes, you didn't show it. Maybe it was because our unusual environment kept us from indulging in feminine frailties. Although sleeping quarters were separate, the rest of our time we shared with men on an equal basis; dressed alike, treated alike (more or less), we were members of the armed forces first; being female was secondary and a lot of the army attitudes rubbed off on the ATS.

No Route Marches were ever posted on Battery Orders at Dalmeny and I, for one, missed them. We still played hockey at home and away and I still suffered in silence each time the match happened to be across the water. Dances too were held as before on alternate Sundays, but the floor had to be treated with French chalk before a dance; we were after all at HQ.

Volunteers were asked for on the 2 p.m. parade for this task. The Orderly Sergeant should have known better than to ask for volunteers for anything, but maybe he knew what he was doing. When no one spoke up, naturally the dancers from our hut eventually did, so it became our unofficial task; we didn't really mind. Discussing the Sunday dance round the fire one night, someone suggested it might be fun to have a Fancy Dress dance. This was enthusiastically agreed upon so Odgers was detailed to ask the Battery Office clerk to put it on the dance notice. We didn't ask permission, we'd soon know whether or not it would be allowed when the orders went on the board, meanwhile we told all the other dancers that the next one would be Fancy Dress.

That was a challenge in itself: costumes would have to be ninety per cent initiative and the rest skill and scrounging ability. Not all bothered to make the attempt or said they couldn't think of anything, but surprisingly on the night most of the girls had concocted something. We hadn't any prizes of course, it was just for fun which seemed in short supply at that time.

Just a week or two before the dance, the ATS had been given the chance to buy from some welfare scheme or other a three-yard length of material supposedly for underwear (civilian). We all took advantage of this, though some of the colours were a bit striking; those days undies were either white or pale shades. Urquhart had bought a length of vivid pea green satin which she had already cut into, so she couldn't make that into anything. She did attend our own dances sometimes.

Another girl had bought a length of pretty blue with bunches of tiny flowers scattered over it, this she wore as a sari. With her dark brown hair, a lipstick caste mark on her forehead, bare legs and bracelets one of the men had made from wire, she looked alluring. Alas, three yards was not long enough for a sari, not to wear to dance a quickstep. With it wound round bra and pants precariously, she spent most of the evening semi-static, but she looked the prettiest. Two others had borrowed scout hats from boys in the railway cottages near the site, scrounged two pairs of ragged fatigue denims from the stores, made one into a cowgirl skirt, the other into cowboy trousers and with the scouts' neckerchiefs, they looked a charming pair from Texas.

I gave myself the most work, I cut my PT shirt up the front, stitched curtain rings on the edges and laced a pyjama cord through to make a bolero, wore a shirt without a collar and sleeves rolled up. For a skirt I stitched two curtains together, gathered round my waist with another pyjama cord. With another borrowed neckerchief, curtain rings dangling from my ears and legs, make up on all exposed skin, I thought I looked like a gypsy, especially with feet shod in black plimsolls.

The pea green satin Urquhart (I never got used to calling her Creighton) was stitching with such diligence not shown when darning socks, turned out to be camiknickers. No lace was there to be bought anywhere, but one of our members taught her how to sew a shell edge round the hems. Small buttons were also unobtainable though she scoured shops on her trips to Edinburgh. One day she came back pleased with some she had managed to get. We laughed; true, they were shaped like ribbon bows but were rather large for their intended use. She took not a bit of notice when we pointed out how uncomfortable they might be and ignored the remarks about chastity belts; she wanted something pretty to wear on leave she said. The rest of us made nighties, the easiest thing to make minus bows, ribbons or buttons.

Church Parade was held in the NAAFI on Sundays as at Merrilees and those of the Roman Catholic faith were allowed out to attend their own church if not on manning duty. Denominations other than Church of England could choose to attend Church parade or not. If they decided not they were given fatigues, so most went along with the rest to the NAAFI.

One Sunday a visiting Padre was taking the service and during the first part of it, though I've forgotten this exact words, he told us that all religions except the Anglican Church were pagan. Lieutenant Dickie Dunt who was Orderly Officer that day stood up, faced the congregation and said that if anyone found the Padre's words offensive then they had permission to leave the service. This they did filing quietly out, Urquhart among them, being Church of Scotland.

Our hut housed Church of England, Church of Scotland, Methodists, Baptists, a non-believer and a Roman Catholic, who lived together without rancour over religion. In fact at one period, four of us used to visit different churches while on 24-hr passes. In all I attended services at a Roman Catholic Church, a Methodist Church and a Salvation Army Church as well as my own. At Dalmeny if we were on a 24-hr pass, on Sunday Atterton, Crisp, Odgers and I liked to attend morning service at the little Dalmeny Church.

On HQ site we were accompanied by a mascot on parades and marching drill. Sapper was a beautiful Great Dane belonging to Major Wheatcroft, our CO. For some reason he seemed to prefer the ATS and walked beside us as we paraded to dining hall or wherever we were marching to. On marching drill he would lope along beside us till he got fed up, then go and sit some distance away keeping us in view as we marched. He was usually at the gate after tea, standing beside the ATS sentry until the evening leave. Girls went down the lane then off he'd go with the first ones, sometimes only going as far as the end of the lane to wait for the next contingent, which he might accompany all the way to the bottom into Queensferry. He was well behaved, never chased anything and if something dared to yap or bark, he just ignored it.

Sometimes Sapper would enter a pub or a cafe in search of ATS. One night at a dance in the Naval Base I was dancing a quickstep with a six-foot Marine on the centre of the floor, when couples around us stopped dancing and were laughing. There, coming toward me, threading through the dancers was Sapper.

Gracefully he stepped over the shiny dance floor, the dancers making a gangway. "Sapper" I said "come on" and led him off the floor, my partner following amid laughter from all sides and ribald comments about horse artillery.

"A friend of yours?" the Marine asked. I explained about the dog as we reached the back of the hall where some of my friends were sitting and told Sapper to stay. The sailors made a fuss of him, but it was the ATS he'd come to find and the minute those sitting got up to dance he set off round the hall to seek someone else in a khaki skirt. He stayed till we left and instead of slipping quietly away as we usually did, six ATS and a Great Dane left the hall to a chorus of Goodnights.

Edinburgh I fell in love with from the start: although I had visited Scottish relations on the west coast before the war, I had never been further east than Glasgow. Apart from its rich heritage and impressive buildings, the entertainment hadn't ground to a halt. Concerts were still being held at the Usher Hall and at other venues, the Zoo was still open, Princes Street and the castle gardens were still to be enjoyed. Lieutenant Emerson (of the dust) managed somehow to get a reduction on concert tickets for us and I have spent many evenings at the Usher Hall enthralled by music. Cpl. Crisp kept all the programmes and those attending the concerts signed their names on the back. The Halle Orchestra I remember particularly. Often our seats would be behind the orchestra. I was glad to sit there because I got a better view of the conductor.

We used to try and book in at a hostel down near the end of Princes Street so that we wouldn't have a long walk after the concert. In the vicinity of the Usher Hall there was also The Silver Slipper Ballroom, very elegant it was too. More expensive than the other dance halls, it was never as crowded, but it could have been the ballroom in an emperor's palace with its rich curtains and velvet-covered gold chairs surrounding the beautiful floor.

Many large dance halls pre-war had revolving stages and that one was no exception; no interval while the musicians had a well-earned break, but non-stop music and plushy comfort if you just wanted to sit and talk. The large silver ball suspended from the ceiling, which threw petals of light over the dancers in the dimmed ballroom while a waltz was playing was romantic. As always we envied the civilian girls in their lovely dresses and glamorous hairstyles, when ours was regulation length above the collar. Whatever we wore, the main thing was that we were dancing to good music, wonderful tunes and enjoying every minute of it. The only fly in the ointment was that some hostels kept early hours, but we didn't have to face a long journey back afterwards and there was the later breakfast time to look forward to. Though even hostels were only one step away from being spartan.

I didn't visit Edinburgh half as often as I would have liked, one 24 hours in Edinburgh I spent full of envy. A manning team from D section were on display for a week outside the Art Gallery in Princes Street. A large anti-aircraft gun was placed along with spotters, Telescope, Height finder and Predictor, to give the public a close-up of the weapons of AA Command and its gunners. It was probably a morale boosting exercise and perhaps a recruiting one, the ordinary rank and file not knowing the reason, they just read Battery orders and complied. Three of us went to visit the team as soon as we stepped off the bus on reaching the city. There they were, surrounded by an interested crowd, some in British uniforms and some in the uniform of our allies. Each one of the team as smart as paint and a credit to the Royal Artillery.

Some time later I saw my name up on Battery Orders for an event even better than standing beside a gun on Princes Street. I was to march along Princes Street. The snag being I was supposed to be starting a 24-hr pass that day at 2 p.m., but the order stated that all personnel chosen for the march the following day would parade in service dress for inspection and marching drill after the 2 p.m. parade.

Only ATS were involved, the person taking the salute was to be HRS the Princess Royal who was Commandant of the ATS. After the inspection some of us were ordered to go to stores and exchange our hats, new ones had recently been issued with hard peaks whereas the original ones had stitched peaks which we preferred. Collecting a new one, I managed to avoid handing in my old hat. This I continued to wear keeping the new one for other official occasions of which there was only one other – a parade with all the other services, again in Edinburgh a little while later.

My diary records the events of the day and preparation. "What a 24 hours, up and down to stores half the afternoon, horrible new stiff brimmed hat, peak too big like a guardsman's, shall not wear it after tomorrow. Drill, Drill, Drill, will need new shoes as well!"

The next day, full of excitement and a tiny bit nervous, even though we were as near perfect as our drill Sergeant could make us, we set off in a truck for the assembly point. The rest of the day was absolutely wonderful and worth missing half my leave for. To march down Princes Street with crowds lining the pavements, led by a Pipe Band with kilts swinging, was unforgettable. The "Eyes Right" as we reached the saluting base was executed with perfect timing. It was worrying at intervals because somewhere behind me was a brass band in the centre of the parade and at the rear another. Faint strains from them wafted to my ears now and then, it needed all my concentration not to lose step. It worried a few of the others they told me later, but the worst didn't happen and the march culminated at St. Giles Cathedral where a service was held. The cathedral was full and the sound of singing voices of the servicemen and women was moving. *The Last Post* was played by a Trumpeter. That day was one of the most memorable in my army career.

The correspondence between the Royal Engineer "somewhere in England" and I at the end of the Forth Bridge in Scotland continued, and when Bob asked me to spend some of my next leave with him at his parents' house I agreed. Our leaves didn't exactly coincide, my leave began before his so I was at home the first part of my nine days. I hadn't told my mother about Bob previously, only in a general way, so she was a little surprised when I told her that I would be going to Yorkshire for a few days of my leave.

She naturally wanted to know a bit more about Bob, who his parents were and so on. I was able to show her a photograph of him, fair, curly-haired with a wide smile. I looked through my wardrobe, which didn't take long, and wondered what on earth I should wear for the important visit? It was only for three days, thank goodness from a clothes point of view, though I would have liked to spend longer with Bob. Of course the others in my hut went to town when they knew about the intended visit and a few lively sessions round the fire followed. Speculations about what the parents would be like, whether we'd get engaged or whether we'd elope: neither of these things happened.

It was arranged for Bob to spend a day with his family before I arrived for three days, returning to my own home where I'd have two days more leave before going back to Dalmeny. The Yorkshire family welcomed me warmly with one exception, Bob's mother. Her words were welcoming but not her eyes. The head of the family and I got on famously. He wasn't as stern as my father and they were allowed to talk at table. One brother was away fighting in the desert, one was a mining surveyor, a reserved occupation, and two were still at Grammar School. Out of that family two were in uniform. Not many homes had sideboards lacking photographs of soldiers, sailors or airmen, some poignantly from the First World War.

It snowed during the night and I remember looking out of my bedroom window the next morning to a world of shining whiteness. Everyone had stayed up talking half the night and no one had woken me, so it was late that Sunday morning as I drew back the curtains. Not a good start, I felt, but no one it seemed had risen early except Dad.

The surveyor was engaged to a girl from the village, she too was in the ATS as a clerk. Stationed fairly near she was able to obtain frequent weekend passes. She happened to be on leave that weekend, along with a cousin of Bob's who was in the RAF. They both turned up after dinner and all of us except the parents went for a long walk. The sun shone on the seven of us as we plodded through the snow, the two younger ones throwing snowballs till in the end everyone joined in.

I decided that I liked Yorkshire. Walking high up on a ridge from which you could see for miles, it was exhilarating and as we all trooped back for tea a trifle damp, everyone glowed. The youngest brother confided in me that he had discovered one of his mother's hiding places and that there would be chocolate biscuits on the tea table. That would be something to look forward to, we agreed. The table was crowded, with nine of us conversation was noisy and there was much laughter. Bob's father had an impish sense of humour. I could see from whom Bob had inherited his. Chocolate biscuits there were and other goodies too.

The evening which followed meant church, for the family were staunch Methodists and I met a whole gathering of family relations there at the evening service. I felt that I was being inspected, however discreetly; not many "foreigners" were brought home by the sons of the village, they tended to court and marry local girls. After church the nine of us walked back up to The Common and a new enjoyable experience for me, an evening round the piano.

All Methodists could sing and did, everyone but me could play the piano but I could sing. Bob's mother had been one of a large family, her father had been the Choirmaster in the next village so they were brought up on a diet of Charles Wesley and some wonderful tunes. I had never taken part in anything other than general hymn singing at church where our choir was male, mainly boys. With Bob's mother seated at the piano, a wonderful wealth of music and voices ensued and I found myself singing descants with confidence by the end of the evening. Because it was Sunday, only hymns were sung, but with what accomplishment! The pianist sang with a strong contralto voice, Dad and the cousin bass, Bob and his elder brother tenor, the boys soprano with the fiancée and myself.

My few days flew by all too quickly and I returned home with plenty to talk about. My mother had a questioning look in her eyes but I couldn't answer her unspoken question, though I supposed I was in a sense courting. Hopefully, Bob would be invited to my home for his next leave, but as soon as I returned to the site it was to find out that all leave for the services had been cancelled till further notice, which sounded ominous.

Meanwhile, those of us who had just returned were called "lucky dogs" by the unlucky ones who were about due for leave. I was put through an intense question and answer session by the ones in my hut. They wanted to know every detail of my visit to Bob's family. Atterton remarked in her Norfolk tongue, "I was sure yo'd come back sporting" (the t was missed out of many of the words so it came out like spor' in) "an engagement ring, I told 'em you would, why di'nt ya? Ya di'nt fall out did ya?" "No we didn't fall out," I said, wondering how much to tell them and how much to leave out. Not that there was anything to tell of the kind of information they were seeking and which I had left my mother wondering about. Bob and I were fond of each other and I'd sampled a bit of Yorkshire life with a close-knit family. We had hardly been alone together and it was an accepted fact that no sitting in the parlour after the others had gone to bed would be allowed. The situation therefore hadn't changed with regard to any future plans and to be honest I wasn't really sure whether I was glad or sorry.

Bob's letters became warmer in content than before, but everyone's future was is the lap of the gods and life so uncertain that I was relieved in a way not to have to make any decisions just then. The lack of a ring for me soon faded into insignificance as more interesting developments were being whispered about and the "second front" filled our minds.

The Predictor team I was in, headed by Cpl. Paterson (soon to be promoted to Sergeant) was sent to Burrowhead on a course to learn about new instruments. As more were produced they would be installed on gunsites to replace the out-of-date ones. The course was long and arduous; no free evenings. We fell into bed at night with no thoughts of the vermin last encountered there.

Time was precious, thousands of operators had to learn the new techniques and teach the rest on site when they returned and the instruments had been installed, which wasn't immediately. Notes and lectures had to suffice in the meantime, which wasn't satisfactory. Tension was mounting in the War Cabinet and among the assembling invasion troops. We felt the ripples even in far away Scotland.

Doodlebug Alley

On the 6th of June 1944, Britain invaded German-occupied France. The "second front" had begun and from then on events intensified. Hitler's secret weapon, the V1 Rocket, was unleashed upon the civilian population in the south of England. The flying bomb could not be aimed at any specific military target, once launched it could not be directed with any accuracy and so was a weapon of reprisal with no military value. The pilotless aircraft were launched across the English Channel, catapulted from a ramp at a speed faster than that of a fighter plane. With flames streaming from their tails, they came like swarms of huge insects with a fiendish noise and when their engines cut out they dived earthwards bringing death and destruction wherever they landed.

At the beginning, many reached London with horrifying results. The Londoners with their usual sense of humour always in evidence throughout the war reduced the frightening robots to comic machines by calling them Doodlebugs. The "Diver" horror though was to last for more than nine months. Many Ack Ack batteries were already in action in the south of England, they had been transported from other defended areas to provide cover for the D-day preparations, so there was a higher percentage of guns than usual already down there. They had to try to stem the flow of Doodlebugs till reinforcements arrived.

Our battery moved into the Diver Belt. It says a lot for the security of the day that the Germans were totally unaware of the facts. Unbeknown to Hitler, nearly every gun in the Royal

Artillery was being deployed in the south of England, desperate situations called for desperate measures.

The uprooting of heavy guns and equipment moving whole batteries from all over Britain was a gigantic operation. Another enormous effort was needed and supplied by the Royal Electrical and Mechanical Engineers (REME). Guns and instruments had to be sited and set up for action as quickly as possible. RA and REME together worked round the clock to install instruments which some of the operators had never even seen. Technical improvements had been taking place steadily throughout the war, but it seemed to us then that everything which had been on the drawing board was hurled into action, us included. It was vastly different from being in action with four guns and others some miles away, to being in a concentrated almost touching line of guns which were never silent for long we found.

We arrived after a long and tiring journey by train which took from 4 p.m. one day till 9.30 p.m. the following day, all faithfully recorded in my diary. We were fed on the train with sandwiches and we had Pay parade on the train. Apart from a party of male gunners who had gone on ahead, the whole Battery was ensconced on the troop train. As soon as we arrived the ATS were set to work, some to prepare a dining room and some to put up beds and collect bedding. Our section was in Seefield House, a boarding school from which its occupants had long since been evacuated. The Battery was not operational for some hours, the gunners hauled and heaved the heavy guns into position. The REME carried out the installation of the instruments and a Tracker tower was built. The new Predictor was called a Tracker and was to be operated from a platform.

Arriving as it was getting dark we had no idea where we were until morning when we were given our new address which sounded odd. We didn't have it for long, as a few days later we were moved down the road to another boarding school, Effingham House, where more scrubbing, cleaning and unpacking stores had to be done.

The first night I was afraid, we all were but no one admitted it. Six of us from the original dozen were sleeping together, the others in the next room. There were no curtains at the windows or blackout shutters, but no light bulbs either. The sky was alight and the noise deafening. The guns were much nearer to our sleeping quarters than ever before so we felt more of the blast when the guns were firing.

One of the rockets landed with an explosion nearby and our windows shattered inwards. We were showered with glass but only two of the girls had minor cuts. As I sat up in bed picking bits of glass off the blankets, I recalled the words of Lieutenant Revill the day that 536 Battery was formed, that we would have to live together, work together and maybe die together. The first two things had come to pass, it looked as if the third might happen soon and I shivered.

The battery next to us was the recipient of the rocket and there were casualties, one of the ATS was blinded. There were more casualties in Ack Ack Batteries as well as among the civilian population, as the months of the Second Battle of London were fought by Ack Ack and Fighter Command. That night the fact that our guns were still silent and the ones on either side of us were blasting away, made me feel vulnerable somehow. If our guns had been in action, even if I hadn't been on manning duty I would have felt better; silly really because the danger wouldn't have been any less.

Once the guns and instruments were operational there was no time for thinking what might happen, all my concentration was needed for the unfamiliar Tracker and new procedures. Each member of the teams carried out their duties in the usual calm, efficient way. We didn't sleep in beds every night so it didn't matter about the windows without glass. When manning, the whole 24-hr period meant staying with instruments and guns, food was brought to us from the cookhouse.

We were part of the Diver Belt which consisted of a compact belt of guns along the south coast. The RAF Fighter planes intercepted targets over the sea; the whole plan was to bring the rockets down into the sea and complicated rules of engagement were laid down. The guns were allowed to fire up to 10,000 yards out to sea and up to 6,000 ft in height. The Fighters were allowed to fly over the guns above 6,000 ft. The rocket was a small target compared to a plane and flew at a high speed. The

Fighters needed a large area to make a kill. Everyone had to adapt quickly to the new equipment; the guns, although the same size, had been modified by the REME to be compatible with our new instruments.

Radar, which we had acquired during our second year, was nothing like the sophisticated set-up that confronted us in the Diver Belt. The first set had been a small cabin which revolved out in the open, a long way from the Command Post, surrounded by a huge steel mesh "mat". The cabin and the "mat" were several feet from the ground. The equipment waiting for the ATS was Plotter and Tracker which compiled much more information than the previous instruments and Remote Control which actually fired the guns. Steel helmets were worn at all times when out of doors: no one needed reminding of this rule for shrapnel rained down most of the time.

Our guns were beside the sea a few miles from Bexhill on Sea. The village of Little Common was nearby and when off duty for an hour or two, we'd walk across the fields to the church hall where a band of ladies served tea and sandwiches, occasionally there would be scones. I never eat cucumber sandwiches without remembering those ladies at Little Common. Their cucumber ones of wafer-sliced white bread were absolutely delicious. After walking in the hot sun, wearing thick skirts, lisle stockings and steel helmets, to enter the coolness of the church hall and be offered such manna was indeed heavenly. I don't suppose the men appreciated the garden-party style of food but they would be cheered by the fact that the ladies were always there smiling behind the teapots. Another blessing in the hall was table tennis and I became quite skilled at the game while we were stationed there.

The Doodlebugs came over continuously so firing was continuous. It was no use waiting till a raid was over, it never was. As we walked, dodging the shrapnel, we would listen for the damnable engines to stop and throw ourselves underneath whatever cover there was if they did.

A bus ran to Bexhill from the village: although the service wasn't very frequent we used it, then sometimes walked back. With so many troops in the area we were often given lifts, more than once I have sat on a pile of ammunition in the back of an army lorry. Everyone in Bexhill was dressed for summer, in peacetime it would have been filled with holiday-makers. Now many of the shops were boarded up, the hotels requisitioned and the beach covered with barbed wire and concrete barriers. The Pavilion at Bexhill still held dances; Urquhart, Stevenson, Odgers and I sampled its ballroom floor once. Little Common held village dances in a hall quite near our billets, so we still managed to dance, though never before had we ever spent time on hairdos, only to have them flattened by a "tin hat" plonked on the top.

One afternoon in Bexhill, Urquhart and I were rooting through a Bargain Box outside a bookshop, when the owner came out and told us that we could take as many books as we could carry from a certain shelf inside the shop for nothing. He was moving his business somewhere a little safer, he informed us. We thanked him warmly for his generosity and wished we had a kitbag with us. However, the booty we arrived back at Effingham House with was much appreciated, even though it didn't exactly enable us to start a Lending Library.

The life there was totally unlike anything we had ever experienced before, no marching drill, fire piquet or ABCA lectures. No time could be spared on those things, it was constant manning on instruments and guns. The timetable was not as before or only loosely similar to the 24-hr routine of gunsites. The periods of manning duty were experimental for a while, the whole operation was so unusual there on the south coast that a standard procedure had not been printed. All the girls had to do spotting duty as well, one trained spotter with an instrument operator on duty together. Later on the men also did spotting duty, each with a trained spotter. It was hot during the months we spent down in the Diver Belt, fortunately, as we spent most of the time out of doors. Fatigues were the only thing that didn't change, washing up and preparing vegetables were the same whether carried out in a field or in a kitchen yard. The daily cleaning of the establishment was carried on whatever battle was raging. The free time when allowed to don service dress and leave the billets was staggered, maybe two hours during a morning, a few in an afternoon, a full evening leave now and again, no 24 hours at all.

One morning after some weeks of such an erratic way of living I was told to pack. Later that day as part of an advance party, I left Effingham House, Little Common, nr. Bexhill on Sea for Ack Ack Command, Somewhere in England. The security was so tight, it's a wonder the address wasn't "Somewhere in Britain".

By army truck we were taken through endless miles of twisting and turning lanes to our new destination in the middle of nowhere, or so it seemed to us. Actually, it was the middle of Romney marsh we later found out, but to us it still appeared to be the middle of nowhere as, dumped with out kitbags, we looked around. It didn't even remotely resemble a gunsite; there weren't any guns for a start, no guardroom to report at, nothing but miles of marsh, us and a great pile of ropes and canvas. This we discovered, to our dismay, was to be our only shelter for an indefinite length of time.

We were not inspired with much confidence for our safety, yet no girl openly voiced her fear. Instead we joked – our usual response to frightening situations – it was our armour against fear. If we could laugh about it we could reduce its strength and it became bearable. Pride also was uppermost, in what we were doing, the uniform we wore, the acceptance of ATS in combat side by side with men against an enemy who had dared to attack Britain. The laughter broke out after the first few moments of apprehension as someone started reading out imaginary newspaper headlines like *Lost in a bog, Marooned in a marsh, Sunk without trace* and other horrifying possibilities. After all, someone else pointed out, we had traversed miles without a sign of any habitation either military or civilian, so what if the drivers, unable to find the right location, had got fed up and just unloaded their cargo anywhere?

No officer accompanied the party, which numbered a Bdr, three male gunners, Sergeant Paterson with her instrument team and a cook. We had been singing on the journey through the lanes but the singing had stopped as we arrived and no one felt like singing any more that day. It was between five o'clock and six, we were all tired, not even a mug of tea could be provided until stores had been unpacked. We had to wait till seven thirty for that mug of tea and the cold meal rustled up by the cook. Meanwhile, facing us was the pile of canvas.

It had never been mentioned at ATS training camp that we'd be required to live under canvas. As for being taught how to erect army tents, that was certainly omitted from any manual. Obviously, it hadn't been envisaged that ATS would ever need to add tent pitching to their list of accomplishments, but then neither was it foreseen that ATS would serve in a combatant role.

"Well you're in the army now," said Sergeant Paterson recalling the RA Sergeant's words of so long ago. A few deep sighs and some groans were heard before we got on with the job. Putting up tents is an art not picked up in a matter of minutes; in fact it eventually took hours and days. It is one thing to erect one tent so that it doesn't immediately fall down, but quite another to erect several in straight lines with the exact number of inches between them, army regulation style. We succeeded in our efforts or so we thought, standing back to survey the results of the past two hours of wrestling with guy ropes, mallets, pegs and yards of canvas endowed with a will of its own. There was no doubt that the tents were decidedly askew. They remained like that until the next morning when the horrified Bdr made us take them down again.

The men were erecting bell tents some distance away from the ATS lines, ours were ridge tents to sleep four. By that time the mist had stealthily crept in with the dusk. Marsh meant mist we learned, cold clinging mist which rolled up every evening, sometimes swirling round ankles, other times just a blanket of grey hanging damply like a curtain. It usually rolled away when the sun arose but was always back when the light began to fade. All that time we had been hearing Ack Ack gunfire which sounded fairly near, though no guns were visible.

As we sat wearily down on a heap of canvas there was a sudden lull in the firing. It felt uncanny and for a while no one spoke, enveloped by the mist in a hushed silence, each thinking her own thoughts. It lasted for a few minutes then inevitably the peace was shattered and once more the sounds of war could be heard.

That night the ATS slept fully clothed in the lorry, steel

helmets clutched on chests. None of us slept much but that we were used to. After there had been one or two near accidents with steel helmets, the Sergeant ordered us to remove them from their protective role and said we'd be safer risking the shrapnel than being wounded by the sharp edge of a steel helmet. Incredible on looking back that we spent the night in a lorry covered with tarpaulin, weaponless on a marsh, not even a pickaxe handle between us. The male gunners were tucked in one of the tents which at least fastened at the entrance, while the fair sex were exposed to whatever may have been lurking in the mist and the marsh. We were all so tired as we lay down that no jokes were forthcoming about possible dangers that night. It was only afterwards that we giggled about it.

Everyone was cold, cramped and crabby after a night in the lorry. It still looked and felt like the middle of nowhere as, peering through the mist, we went in search of breakfast. Some hard work was in store for us erecting sleeping accommodation, dining marquee, MI tent, offices, Sergeants' and Officers' Mess tents and kitchen. We dug latrines too, they were trenches screened by a rough framework covered with sacking, later the ATS were given chemical toilets. No water supply was on site, it had to be brought. The ATS had beds: low, light wooden folding ones. If care wasn't taken they could collapse beneath you. Duck boards also were supplied, the marshy ground being always damp. When it rained it was a mire.

The Battery arrived two days later with guns and instruments. Soon it was in action, hurling its bursting shells into the sky at the still oncoming VI rockets. The magnitude of General Pile's operation in gun power had paid off as later figures and reports proved, none of which was known to us at that time. We only knew that we were doing, to the best of our ability, the task which we had been trained to do. If the girls had thought life with the RA was rough before, it got rougher, but we grumbled through it all, we joked through it all and we came through it all.

Guns and instruments were manned round the clock and, as at Little Common, the Spotting duty was shared by all. Experimenting still went on with lengths of duty periods which were always being changed at first. Eventually it was decided that sections would man guns and instruments for the specified 24 hours, but broken up into 8 hours off and 8 hours on. Sandwiches and tea were carried to the teams at their posts. Of course fatigues were done as usual, well not quite as usual, potatoes were peeled dry, vegetables were not cleaned as thoroughly, neither was crockery. At the time we never gave a thought to the cooks but it must have been hard for them, the acute shortage of water and being without a kitchen.

I think the water situation hit us the hardest, the ATS anyway. Needless to say water was rationed, it was delivered every third day to the site, the individual ration was meagre. The men saved the cold tea dregs to use for shaving. After washing and teeth cleaning (this in the sleeping tent, no toilet facilities in camp), we would save the used water and, lacing it with Dettol, wash our shirts and undies. They took ages to dry in the tent, it wasn't allowed to hang washing out. Laundry was collected, but like many other things at that time, was spasmodic, so it was considered safer to wash our own. The possibility of using water from the dykes crisscrossing the marsh had been considered by the ATS, but on closer inspection the risk of causing an epidemic of cholera or worse was too great, so the idea was abandoned.

Eventually baths were organised; at least baths were mentioned and one day when the first Bath Parade was mustered, our section was on it, we whooped with joy and foolishly expected baths. Climbing into the truck, the ATS were clutching towels, soap and whatever bathtime luxuries they used on special occasions and of course that was a special occasion. Singing "I'm forever blowing bubbles" and "I shall be whiter than the whitewash on the wall," we arrived at the camp of a Tank Regiment. Driven through the gate, we were unloaded outside a large, high, brick building without windows. Ushered inside by the accompanying NCO, the door locked behind us, we looked around – no baths could be seen. A long row of fixed showerheads, high up without curtains or cubicles, a concrete floor with drains, a single tap at one end which turned all the showers on or off.

On the wall at the opposite side was a row of hooks and that was our dream of wallowing in a bath gone west. At least there was water. It was impossible to prevent hair from getting wet and those with curled coiffures were hesitant about standing underneath. There was no way of adjusting the spray, they were too high to reach. As we stood looking quietly round, the NCO said, "Come on, hurry up, we haven't all day, clothes off and under the showers." Quickly we obeyed. Showering was new to most of us, in those days they were still a novelty. Once over the initial shock about the lack of baths and privacy, we abandoned all decorum and ran naked down the line of showers through the spray like nymphs, hair streaming, playing follow my leader until suddenly the flow of water stopped.

The NCO was standing beside the tap. "What do you think you are playing at?" she said when there was silence, "It sounds just like a school playground in here, no one would guess that you were gunners. Now I'm giving you two minutes more under the showers and I want everybody dressed and lined up beside that door in five." Subdued but sparkling clean, we were lined up by the stated time and on our return gleefully shattered the hopes of the rest, planning foam baths and the like by telling them the bare facts of the Bath Parade.

There was unrationed water in the camp, below the camp really, for it was in the bottom of the slit trenches which had been dug for our safety all over the place. Non-manning personnel were supposed to take shelter in the nearest one if a rocket cut out above us, but safety was questionable regarding those trenches. People fell into them without intending to. Placed haphazardly here and there, or so it appeared, though there may have been a master plan drawn by an army draughtsman, our trenches were dug by our men without a plan. Not being used to trenches, we forgot they were there half the time. Miraculously there were no broken bones.

One day a male gunner carrying a pile of newly delivered laundry, not being able to see over the bundles of shirts and socks, disappeared into a trench, the clean shirts flying in all directions, most of them following the hapless gunner into the mud at the bottom. To those of us who witnessed the mishap it was sheer slapstick and needless to say we laughed long and loud before anyone moved to rescue the unfortunate fellow. Luckily, he didn't do himself any lasting damage but he had provided a tonic for all. Laughter is a tonic and a lot more laughter was heard as the incident was retold by the ones who had witnessed it.

Until the supply ran out, the ATS apparel emitted a strong aroma of eau de Dettol and though shirts and collars were reasonably clean, they had a wilted look. Of course we were supposed to send them on the laundry truck and when they returned they would be clean and pressed. The uncertainty of delivery, however, would still mean wearing wilted shirts while awaiting the visit of the laundry truck. At least washing our own made sure that the wilted shirts were clean.

Podge somehow, in the desolate wilderness, made the acquaintance of a kind lady living in a small cottage about half a mile away from our camp. Telling the twelve of us, who were now divided into three tents but still very much a single unit, about the lady she had met, she got up from the bed she'd been sitting on and with a beaming smile at us all said, "Oh, and by the way we can go to her house to do our ironing." Podge had it all worked out; she and one of us taking it in turns would go during the daytime, taking whatever washing was dry.

The cottage had no electricity, we used flat irons heated on an open fire. I can remember sitting in that kitchen awaiting my turn with the iron. It was stifling hot even with the door and window wide open, the flies buzzing and Podge thumping the iron down on the table. She had never used a flat iron before and thought the harder she thumped, the smoother would be the garment. I told her that she was more likely to wear the shirts out using the iron than by wearing them, not to mention the damage to the table.

At first we hung our clothes on tent poles but they always ended up on the duck boards, so it was easier to keep everything in kitbags. When the iron came into our lives, someone devised a method of hanging shirts securely to the pole and after the effort of walking and standing in a hot kitchen, we all took extreme care when occupying the tent. Our clothing had a perpetual dampness about it, even that which had been properly dried at the laundry. After a few days in the tent you couldn't tell which had come from the laundry and which had been hanging to dry for days. Though days were hot, the evenings and mornings were chilly and damp with the eternal mist.

Several weeks passed before our second Bath Parade, a different location in a different direction some way behind the gun belt among the barrage balloons. The WAAF quarters to which we were led were wooden huts with six beds in each, pretty bedspreads, curtains to match, a chest of drawers with a mirror, a mat on the floor and an adjoining bathroom! Though we envied them their luxury, not one of us would have changed places with a WAAF.

The Platform on which the ATS manned the instruments was twelve feet high, a canvas chute led from this down to a slit trench. During lulls in the firing, sometimes we would be given the order to "Take cover" in practice. That meant sliding down the chute into the trench to check how quickly the teams could vacate the Tracker Tower and was the procedure to be followed when a rocket's descent on the top of us seemed imminent. At the previous Command Post the Tracker Tower was new to us, but we got used to climbing up and down. On the marsh we had to get used to the slit trench which we weren't too keen on, nor the method of entering it with its bed of mud. If you slid down as fast as you were supposed to, the part of anatomy used suffered a burning sensation. If you steadied yourself with hands on the sides of the chute as a brake, you ran the risk of a damaged spine by a pair of studded army boots from the person behind you. All in all, climbing down the scaffolding, supporting the tower and sheltering underneath would have been a better plan, so thought the ATS. Hague was one of the first to experience the escape route, she told us that the officer on duty with her said the most important thing she must remember was to protect the binoculars as they cost £40.

The days of inspecting sleeping quarters with their neat pile of blankets, kit layouts and the order "Stand by your beds" had long since gone. Beds were occupied in the daytime by those trying to snatch a couple of hours sleep which seemed impossible until sheer exhaustion took over. Gunners coming off duty, some going on, we slept with steel helmets over faces, on chests or somewhere near to hand, shrapnel could be deadly.

One day the sleepers in our tent were hurriedly awakened and told to get out on parade. We were to put on battledress over pyjamas, steel helmets on top of curlers, push feet without socks into boots and in typical RA tradition we did, it was second nature to obey swiftly without question. The time was 11.30 a.m. (my diary states). Except for the teams manning guns and instruments, the whole Battery was assembled on the grass.

General Pile, for that was who stood before us, told us to "Stand easy" and sit down if we wished, he had something important to say to us. To the rank and file he had only been a name up till then, the Commander in Chief of Ack Ack Command, the sunny day on the marshes he became real to us.

He apologised to those who had been in bed, but said that he wanted to thank us all personally for our efforts in the battle. "Make no mistake," he said, "it is the second battle of London." He then went on to give percentages of targets destroyed so far by Ack Ack and talked of our hardships and our problems (technical and otherwise), which all of us were having to contend with and were still trying to overcome.

A pep talk we called it afterwards, discussing the day we had paraded before a General in pyjamas and curlers, but it was more than a pep talk. Though we made the usual fun of anything serious, it was a tremendous boost to our morale. The fact that all our training and experience had stood the critical test when in the front line of Britain's defence, was satisfying to say the least and I am sure that everyone listening to the General that summer day was aware of the sincerity of his thanks.

Sadly missed was the NAAFI whose services we had been deprived of for so long. A WVS van called once and there was a lengthy queue for tea, buns, writing paper, combs and whatever else was on board. One other visit especially welcomed by the ATS was from a man who owned a Chemist's shop, he must have got security clearance to be on the site. From the boot of his car he sold toothpaste, medicines, shampoos and cosmetics which were almost unobtainable then. Most were unbranded but nevertheless welcome. He was fair and rationed us so that the ones in the front of the queue couldn't buy the lot. I bought some face cream, that is what the label said, but on inspection it didn't look like cream. Doubtful about its content, I didn't use it and much later when on leave I gave it to my cousin to analyse. He said it was 90% shaving cream and used it for that purpose.

Thomas of D Section (she of the Release Form) bought some henna hair dye and couldn't wait to experiment with it till she went on leave, the reinstatement of leave being in the lap of the gods. Thomas scrounged all the used water she could and saved it, begging each day till she thought she had enough. By then it didn't look any cleaner than the stuff in the dykes which surrounded us. Resting outside in the shade of the tent one hot afternoon, three of us had escaped into a world of fiction, each lying or sitting on the grass, immersed in a book. When we heard shrieks and peals of laughter coming from the direction of D lines, naturally we hastened with all speed to seek the cause of such merriment and what a sight met our eyes! If it hadn't been for the near hysterical laughter, the situation would have indeed appeared grave. Dressed in battledress trousers and bra, surrounded by a group of helpless females, Thomas was bending over an overflowing bowl of what appeared to be blood. The grass all around looked as if a rather gruesome murder had taken place.

The henna might have been expected at worst to give the user a rusty look, but the colour of Gunner Thomas's head was definitely not rusty but blood red. There wouldn't have been enough water in the camp to wash all the dye out. All who had assisted in the operation were smeared with red too. It was several days before the redhead lost her red face, literally. The practice of wearing steel helmets at all times was a blessing for the unfortunate girl as they concealed more of the head than the ATS hats.

Never had hot water been more necessary. Hot water was only a memory, indeed soon after that the daily ration was reduced to one pint per day due to the vast number of troops on the marshes. Before the colour experiment, D Section girls had told us of the new fair method they had devised for the use of their water ration. The four in each tent took it in turns to wash their faces in a small amount of water, then other parts of the anatomy were treated in turn, which meant that every fourth day each girl had clean water for her face.

The mail came to us with its good and its bad news, longed

for letters sometimes arrived, sometimes, never, but always there was hope. We had no address, just the Battery number and Ack Ack Command. We had been issued on our arrival in the Diver Belt with On Active Service envelopes. We stamped and addressed our outgoing letters in the usual way, up to three could be enclosed on the OAS envelope which then went to a base centre for censorship. The letters were posted on from the base. We also, at the same time, were given a card to fill in. These were collected and taken back to Battery Office for any emergency, we guessed.

Active Service Envelope

(Crown Copyright Reserved). A.F. W2076
ACTIVE SERVICE
ARMY PRIVILEGE ENVELOPE
J.D. & Co. Apsley.
INSTRUCTIONS.

1 Up to three letters may be forwarded in this cover, but these must all be from the same writer. The cover should be addressed in such cases to the Base Censor.
2   This envelope must not be used for coin or valuables. It cannot be accepted for registration.
3 Correspondence in this envelope need not be censored regimentally. The contents are liable to examination at the Base.
4 The following Certificate must be signed by the writer.

I certify on my honour that the contents of this envelope refer to nothing but private and family affairs.

Signature
Name etc.
ADDRESS:-

_____

_____

_____

_____

The cards were printed field cards usually issued to soldiers, bearing words such as *I am alive and well, I am at a Base hospital, I am wounded, I am a prisoner of war*, the cards had to be signed. Another opportunity for the witty ones to remark on, we got a few laughs out of the field cards but thankfully we never saw them again.

Many of the ATS received mail on Mail days owing to the ever growing circle of pen-friend letters we wrote. Bob's letters came with regularity, he was still in Europe with the 2nd Army. We were getting to know each other through the written word, numerous courtships were conducted by letter. I received lots of mail but the handwriting I searched for first was Bob's.

Gales started in September: furiously they swept across the marsh and the rain lashed down turning green grass into brown mud. Nothing inside the tents was dry and it was cold. The hot summer days were over. ATS were issued with fly sheets for tents; our problem was to get them up. We battled through the rain and wind with frozen fingers, crying with frustration and cursing whoever should have ordered fly sheets before the gales arrived.

A bright gleam came into our lives one day in the form of an invitation to a dance from 418 Battery. I was one of the lucky ones off duty, the male battery provided transport to take us and bring us back. We climbed into the truck as excited as if we were going to a grand ball instead of just to a marquee on a marsh.

Our hosts even provided a bar, which served only lemonade and beer, but there was music – live music, wonderful music. The band had unfair competition from the howling wind which blew round and through the canvas. The ropes creaked, the canvas flapped the whole time, then suddenly one corner of the marquee came crashing down on the dancers. One ATS was badly cut and taken to hospital. We felt extremely sorry for her on two counts, one that she was hurt at all and the other because, like the rest of us, she had been in the thick of it without getting a scratch and her first battle scars were from a tent pole.

The same night our mess tent blew down and in the morning the men fought with the wind to put it up again while the girls rescued plates from the mud before any breakfast could be served.

Gradually, the rocket launching sites along the French coast were overrun by our troops and demolished by the bombers, so the raids on the south coast trailed off. Our Intelligence reported that Germany was planning to launch rockets from aircraft. Longer range rockets (the VIIs), had already landed in Britain. Some batteries were moved round to the east coast, another gigantic upheaval took place. Other batteries were moved to expected target areas, all with their new or modified equipment.

Our battery was ordered to the north east, back to the site we had left in early summer at the end of the Forth Bridge. The men, guns and instruments went by road after dismantling everything, leaving the marsh to the wind and the rain. In the meantime the ATS were told to quickly pack and board lorries to be taken to Rye into billets where hot water awaited us and a solid roof over our heads. It was so unexpected we didn't know what we had done to deserve it and I for one thought it was too good to be true. I didn't really feel comfortable about things, it was so far removed from the kind of life we had grown used to. All my questions went unanswered, why and for how long none of the NCOs knew, only ATS personnel went to Rye. It was the first time since the Battery was formed that we hadn't all been together and it felt distinctly odd.

Interlude

O ur billets in Rye were requisitioned houses scattered about the town. By the look of them they had been empty for some time. Part of C Section was housed in Market Street quite near to the vicarage, also requisitioned and which served as our cookhouse and mess. The first thing we were ordered to do when reaching our new homes was, as usual, into fatigue dress, report to stores for mops, buckets and whatever happened to be available for cleaning purposes.

Among all the other skills we had acquired in our army career, the one which would be of most value in civilian life was surely the ability to improve any circumstance, to transform any place into a clean spot to lay our heads. In that house, floors and stairs were scrubbed, windows, brass handles and doorknobs shone. The kitchen was given a spring-clean even though we couldn't use it, to cook in that is. We did the ironing there and used it as a wash place when the bathroom was occupied.

The ones cleaning the kitchen opened the back door after a struggle and shouted to the rest of us to come and look. The garden had gone wild and was right up to the door. The reason they had opened the door was to find the outside drain in which to empty the filthy water. It was found eventually, but a lot of undergrowth had to be cleared away from the outside wall with only hands for tools before it was located. As for any hopes of sweet-smelling lines of washing billowing in the breeze, those were dashed when we realised it would take months to clear the jungle, which was shoulder high.

Apart from fatigue denims, service dress was worn at all times. We were marched to and from meals and to cookhouse fatigues as well as to fatigues in other buildings. Every evening was free except for those on cookhouse fatigues, it was so unusual. We talked about it among our own group, still together though not in the same rooms, and all agreed that we could get used to an easy life such as we were living, but the answer to the big question "why?" none of us could fathom.

The house was bare of furniture except for the beds, which had been brought from the marsh; clothes were hung on hooks, some rooms had built-in cupboards. Room inspection began, stripped beds with three biscuits topped by the neat square pile of blankets was again the order. The NCO in charge of each dwelling was responsible for girls checking in at night and Lights Out.

Each morning at breakfast one of us would put the question to an NCO, "When would we be rejoining the Battery?" till one morning an angry Sergeant told me to stop pestering. That was an order she said and the next person to ask would find themselves on a charge for disobeying an order. That was that, but later on from an undisclosed source came news that our spell in Rye would be a matter of days only. The task of moving everything, with many batteries using the roads at the same time in the second mass evacuation to other target areas, and of re-establishing sites as before, was expected to take some days. Security would be the reason why we weren't informed officially, we realised, but knowing the situation enabled us to settle down to enjoy our few days in Rye.

To our delight we were given short free periods during the day in between fatigues, with strict instructions not to hang about the main streets or shops or walk about in large groups. In other words we were to stay out of sight and out of trouble. If any of us contravened this order then the privilege would be taken away from everyone.

I found Rye a fascinating place. Once a busy port, the harbour had been silted up for years, quaint streets full of ancient buildings, a castle and a monastery, the whole town was steeped in history. Though the country was at war, it seemed to have by-passed that little spot. There sitting in the churchyard of Rye Parish Church with Odgers one day, a faint gleam of sun showing through greyish clouds, we indulged again in our "let's pretend it's peace time" fantasy.

All the buildings we could see in the square were old, to our right was the Carmelite Friary. When much of the town was burned down by the French five centuries ago, built of stone, it survived. The building of course was only a portion of the original, which would have enclosed the chapel and hostelry, giving hospitality to travellers, some of whom came from the port. The Carmelites took their name from Mount Carmel when they first established the order in 1155. Some emigrated to England and a Monastery at Newenden, ten miles from Rye, was established in the middle of the thirteenth century. The Friary in Church Square was in connection with that and was used to lodge the Friars as they went about the area collecting gifts from wealthy people, for in those days they were dependent on charity for their support.

We walked through the churchyard and turned left to the nearby remains of Ypres Castle, built in stone in 1135 to protect the town. The sea at the time reached its lower walls. We enjoyed an extensive view from its high position until the cold, damp marsh wind moved us on, thankful that we weren't out there, for those last weeks under canvas had been grim. The church was built in the twelfth century and has undergone many changes. The clock, said to be the oldest going with its original works, had a peculiar pendulum hanging down inside the church.

Conduit Hill descended steeply to Cinque Ports Street; about halfway down on the right-hand side was The Old Monastery. Odgers and I, taking advantage of our free time that day, were charmed by the old town with every step we took and which we probably would never have visited under ordinary circumstances. The Old Monastery, so called, was the Chapel of Friars Heremites of St Augustine, the first Archbishop of Canterbury. They were originally hermits and were first congregated into one body by Pope Alexander IV in 1265. The building was supposed to have been erected in the fifteenth century, but it appeared that the hermits resided there before that.

A lengthy document states:

> *Gift and confirmation by the Mayor and Barons of Rye to the Prior and Brethren of the Order of Friars Heremites of St Austin of the Convent of Rye, of all that place called 'Le Haltone" saving to us a competent space near to the foss for building the wall of our town and a way to go to such wall. In witness whereof we have caused our common seal to be set. Given at Rye on Thursday the Feast of the Translation of St Thomas The Martyr in the second year of Richard, after the conquest of England, the Second.*

The seal is that of the Friars, St Augustine with crozier and an anchor and people standing below. Date 2 Richard II, 1379.

Of course, at the dissolution of monasteries by Henry VIII, Rye suffered the same fate as the rest, but some of the Order remained until the reign of Edward VI who enforced the acts of Henry. It has had various uses since then; a refuge for fleeing French Protestants, a theatre, a malthouse, a salt and provision store, a wool warehouse and others. Just before the Great War the lower floor was a Salvation Army Barracks, the upper apart was an artist's studio, then later used as a Sunday school and let for social functions. While we were in Rye it was used for concerts and dances – a notice to that effect was posted outside. Apart from all the history we learned that day and were eager to share with our friends, the most interesting to them was the last bit.

The concert was the following night and a crowd of us went and enjoyed the Piano Recital given by a Russian lady. A dance was to be held the following night – more our style we all agreed. The Russian lady had played some rather heavy stuff: one of the girls remarked, "Good she may have been but we needed bright stuff." Well she got her bright stuff the next night, the band played all our favourite tunes! We found it a little strange on the dance floor though, it sloped up away from the stage, fine for concert seating but hard on the calf muscles when dancing. We all grumbled the next morning about our aching legs.

In an old book I found a verse dedicated to Rye, which I copied in my autograph book. It reads:

There's a quaint little hill of red roofs
and the gleam of a quaint little church is the crown.
There are castles and cobbles and gateways so grim
its houses are all tumble down,
but this quaintness so sweet makes a picture complete
from the road to that quaint little town.

When three days had passed without any orders to pack I began to get restless again. The others told me to shut up and enjoy it while it lasted and we all went to the cinema that evening to see *The Way Ahead*. During the morning I had noticed a poster on a wall asking for volunteers, needed for temporary work on the land. Due to the shortage of labour, the danger of rockets, the gales and storms, much of the harvest was still out on the marsh. A lot of it was ruined but hands were needed to salvage whatever could be saved and to clear the ground ready for the next sowing of grain.

I remembered the time I had wanted to be a land girl, so decided to try and talk some of my cronies into volunteering for land work. The non-operational existence, although pleasant, was neither one thing or the other and I felt like a piece of surplus army equipment. When I tried telling the others how I felt, I got the usual cries about not volunteering for anything and that I was never satisfied. Why couldn't I just go from day to day in blissful ignorance? We were in ignorance, not being in the midst of things, not knowing how the war was going, not having access to a wireless set (not that we ever did have). The Pathe News at the cinema, though greatly enjoyed, was not up-to-date news.

Odgers agreed with me after a while and I knew that with her on my side it was "in the bag", so the next day two of us headed for the Land Army office with our list of volunteers. We had decided by a majority vote that it would be no use asking permission first from our army. If they were as desperate for labour as the poster suggested, it was up to the Land Army lot to pull strings. Our strategy worked and, to cut a long story short, the next day after breakfast a fair number of new land girls dressed in army denim fatigues collected packets of sandwiches from the cookhouse. A real Land Army girl arrived driving a tractor, towing a long flat trailer, our transport to the marshes. The Sergeant supervising our departure gave us a little lecture, no singing through the streets, obey the Land Army girl whatever she ordered us to do and to remember, above all, that we represented 536 (m) HAA Battery RA.

On our first day it was dry and sunny, some were put to work stacking bundles of grain which, if it dried quickly, would be of use; others raked the ruined crop, which they burned. Both tasks needed stamina as the hours went by in the hot sun. The weather appeared to have taken a turn for the better and stayed that way for two days. The lunch break was welcomed with relief by all, as with scratched arms and blistered hands we sat to eat our sandwiches, all identical so there was no swapping. The chatter wasn't quite so animated as on the journey out, most of it was directed at the girl who had driven the tractor and was in charge of us. Questions about the Land Army, where she was billeted, wages, time off, discipline and so on.

Her name was Marion and she was almost a larger version of Podge, short brown curly hair, rosy cheeks and wide smile. I could easily imagine her in a large kitchen, surrounded by loaves of newly baked bread, the wife of some lucky farmer in the future. She hadn't anyone particular in mind she told us on being questioned, and we were surprised to find that she lived at home in Rye. That sometimes happened in the Land Army she informed us. Privately we all thought that the word "army" was incorrect. How intolerant we were when young.

At the end of that first day on the marsh as we all climbed wearily on to the trailer, Marion showed no sign of tiredness. Helping the last ones up on to the trailer she stood back and surveyed the load of harvesters with a grin. "Well, you don't look as smart as you did when we set off! You'd better take the straw out of your hair and pull your shirt sleeves down to cover the scratches. I can't take you back looking like a bunch of scarecrows." We looked around and laughed; she was right. We began picking bits of straw from each other, just like monkeys at the zoo, someone remarked. Marion said as she was climbing into the tractor, "By the way, there is a dance on at our church hall tonight if anyone is interested."

Tiredness vanished like magic from those who had dancing

feet, as we clamoured to know where and what time, and as the tractor moved over the grass the singing began. We quietened down as we reached the town, hoping that we wouldn't be seen in our grubby sweaty state by any prospective dance partners. If any had seen the load on the trailer, they wouldn't have connected it with the bevy of beauties at the dance that evening. Smart as always with shining buttons, shoes, hair and shining faces a little sunkissed, we danced and danced. Before Marion had uttered the magic words, all we could think of was a bath and bed, but with music like *In the Mood* and *Chattanooga Choo Choo* hidden reserves of energy welled up. Marion was at the dance wearing a cotton dress, I still visualised her in a farmhouse kitchen.

The next morning was a different story as groans emitted from the harvesters about aching muscles. Long after the Rye interlude a few girls admitted that one day in the Land Army had been enough for them but pride, that powerful emotion, enabled them to go on. The weather changed again on the third day to cool and showery. Once or twice when the rain was really heavy, Marion would tell us to run for shelter underneath a corrugated tin-roofed barn.

The liaison between the two authorities was never revealed; we supposed that when our marching orders arrived our harvesting days would be over, but until then we were committed to our voluntary task. What strings were pulled and by whom we never knew and at that time we were not concerned with whys and wherefores, only satisfied that our request had been so speedily complied with. Six days did we toil before we were informed while parading for the evening meal that the next day the ATS of 536 were rejoining the Battery.

After the meal, the ones bearing scratches and blisters, namely those appendaged to the Land Army, were instructed to report to the Land Army office the next morning at 10.00 hrs, attired in service dress, not fatigue denims. When we asked the reason why, the NCO answered that she had given an order and it was to be obeyed. Speculation ensured among us as to the reason for the summons. Would it be for a medal? To recruit our services for the Land Army permanently? Weren't we needed as gunners any more? We wondered all evening about it and now and again someone in our house came up with another possibility; these got sillier as they went on.

All this was revealed when we duly reported to the office the next day at the appointed time. Alphabetically, names were read out and each one of us received a small packet. It was Pay parade. "Glory be!" we hadn't expected that, fancy getting paid twice, for that is what it amounted to. After our first elation, doubts then began to creep in, whether we would in fact be paid by our own army as usual. Pay day was always on a Thursday, but we had been told that ATS pay would be kept at Battery Office until we rejoined the men.

The rest of the day passed quickly with fatigues, packing and cleaning. The house looked as bare as it did when we entered it ten days before. But for the fact that the brass handles gleamed and there wasn't a speck of dust about, you wouldn't know that anyone had been living there. We paraded for an early tea at the Vicarage, sandwiches and army slab cake, which appeared at intervals, always yellow and always dry. We ate it as we ate everything put before us, none of us had ever suffered from food poisoning eating in an army mess.

At 17.00 hrs we marched away from the Vicarage to the railway station. On the order "Fall Out" we each had to collect our own kitbag from an army truck then wait. Another thing we had learned in the army was how to wait. You just made yourself comfortable on whatever was available for sitting on before someone beat you to it. If they did, you sat on the ground and avoided looking at the time. A group of blessed WVS ladies were at the station with gifts of chocolate and biscuits for the journey. Lots of people had numerous reasons for being grateful for the Women's Voluntary Service, including us. Our troop train finally steamed out of Rye station at dusk.

Guns In Glasgow

It was October and the second rocket attack had begun in earnest. A heavy belt of guns was still along the south coast but more batteries were being employed south east and northwards when it was discovered that Holland was where the new V2s were being launched. The new rocket was larger than the flying bomb, it had a much longer range and carried in its warhead 2000 lbs of explosives. The launching platforms were smaller and harder to detect so less were destroyed by bombing. It was expected that the new rockets might reach the north east and even to cities inland.

Some of the most bitter fighting of the war had taken place at Arnhem. The Eighth Army had captured the Italian seaport of Rimini, several French Channel ports had been liberated, allied troops had landed in Greece and battles were still raging in the Far East. There was good news and bad news that autumn and we were in the sixth year of the war.

It was 15.30 hrs the day after leaving Rye when the ATS set foot on the gunsite they had left in the summer and life carried on as before. Battery Orders were perused as soon as we had changed into battledress to discover the D Section were on manning duty and our section was on fatigues. Some names were listed for evening leave, my name among them and off I went to the dance at the Roseberry Hall.

The months we had been away sometimes felt like a dream for we picked up the threads doing everything we did before. Leave was started again, those who had waited the longest were top of the list, mine was granted in November. Bob's parents had invited me to visit them and I spent a few days in Yorkshire. We all went to the Leeds Empire theatre to see Oscar Rabin and his Band and, another evening, to the cinema to see *Song of Bernadette*. Bob was still overseas.

Lieutenant Emerson had started his lectures again and we learned more of the situation abroad. With nearly every country in the world involved in the war it was a sobering thought. No jokes were ever heard in the lecture rooms during those talks of strategy and policies of the governments concerned. That office also tried to arrange courses for us on various subjects from the Army Education Service, everyone in our hut put their names down for something.

A long list of subjects was posted up, Shorthand and Typing, Bookkeeping, Catering Management and Crafts were only a few. Some of the girls were quite excited, not those from our hut. With our usual ability for looking on the black side, doubting that anything good would come our way, we were not too disappointed when nothing came of Lieutenant Emerson's plan. Knowing him, we were sure it would not be through his lack of trying.

Corporal Crisp came back from leave to tell us how much she had enjoyed spending time with one of her cousins who had leave at the same time. She hadn't seen him since he joined the RAF, which was before she had joined up. At a family gathering the RAF cousin had sung a song to Crisp while dancing, which amused her. She asked him to write it down for her, then she brought it back to us as she didn't think we knew that particular RAF song. She was correct in her thinking, none of us had heard it before. It went in my autograph book along with another verse which Crisp had copied from a magazine and thought appropriate. Just before her leave we'd had a serious talk from Lieutenant Emerson about the war situation.

The serious one reads:

> *We shall look back on those great things come the peaceful years.*
> *We shall look back remembering the trials, the toil, the tears.*

We shall look back in wonder as we go our quiet ways
and marvel at the mighty efforts of this present phase.
So long as man can write and speak, the story will be
heard
and generations yet to come, will listen and be stirred
by the final shattering of German pride and power,
the things that now are happening this day, this very
hour.

The second one did cause merriment and of course we sang it round the fire. It was a parody of the song "Are you lonesome tonight".

Are you lonesome tonight, is your brassiere too tight,
are your corsets all falling apart?
Does the size of your chest wear big holes in your vest,
does your spare tyre reach up to your heart?

Are your stockings all laddered and shoes wearing
thin,
do you hold up your bloomers with a big safety pin?
Are your false teeth all worn, do they drop when you
yawn?
then no wonder you're lonesome tonight

Stevenson remarked that the reason we had never heard it before was because the RAF only sung it to the WAAFs they danced with. They would never dare to sing it to one of us.

One of the officers obviously thought that we were settled for a time at Dalmeny and decided to keep a few ducks. Water for them to paddle in was provided by an old tin bath. Their stay with us was not a lengthy one; at the beginning of December the Battery moved to Glasgow, C and D Sections to Baillieston right beside a canal. When the ducks were unloaded they made straight for the water and were last seen swimming south.

The first night there we had an air raid, I was on manning duty and when the alarm sounded I turned right on leaving the hut, which was the direction to the Command Post at Dalmeny. I had forgotten, being only half awake, that we had moved that day and if it hadn't been for the moonlight shining on the canal, I would have been in it. The thought of what nearly happened stayed with me for a long time and I was always afraid that I might forget, on a night raid, to go left instead of right.

Just a little way along the road from the site was a school with the name Happidrome on the gate. A few of us were curious about it so we made enquiries. We found out it was a school for handicapped children and we asked permission to visit. The staff made us welcome and we visited a number of times while we were stationed there. Christmas was near and discussions went on in our hut about the possibility of doing something for the children. A few suggestions were put forward but the best one, we all agreed, was to hold a party for them in our NAAFI.

Of course there were all the "ifs" to consider. Would the officers give permission? Would the cooks prepare the party food? Would the NAAFI staff allow us to use the canteen for a children's party? A unanimous "yes" from all sides was the response, to our delight, and swift plans were put into operation. From then onwards an amazing number of helpers were busy on tasks of a non-military nature.

Men made toys from wood, paint and bits of things from stores. Many of us had wool and odd scraps of material left over from one thing or another and we made soft toys. Dolls, rabbits, clowns, were a few I remember, much ingenuity and creative skill was displayed. Some of the grey rabbits were suspiciously like our socks and there was a bigger demand than usual from the MI room for certain packets which were used for toy stuffing. The medical orderly residing in our hut wasn't entirely happy about it when she discovered the fact, but resignedly closed her eyes, metaphorically speaking.

The head of the school had supplied a list with every child's name, and the presents (each bearing a name tag) arrived at the canteen door where a bunch of excited children waited at the end of the party. Santa Claus, alias Captain Funell, rode majestically towards the steps of the canteen seated on the top of a utility truck amid loud cheers from us all, ours louder than the children's. The whole enterprise had been a huge success, consequently Christmas itself was a bit of an anti-climax.

Within walking distance of the site, as well as Happidrome,

was a hospital, and some of us thought it would be good idea to sing carols on Christmas morning round the wards. Quite a number of our male gunners were Welsh, and Church Parades, therefore, were notable for the singing as were the route marches at Merrilees. Their rendering of *Guide me oh thou Great Jehova* was unforgettable and on occasions when it is sung at a service which I am attending, it is our combined voices I always hear, the voices of C and D Sections 536 (m) HAA Bty, not those around me.

One of the regular Sergeants was heard to say on more than one occasion, "If the bloody Taffys worked as well as they sang we'd have the best mob in the British army." The men, however, including the Taffys, were disinclined to join us in hospital visiting, always supposing we were allowed by both authorities to do so. One of our number, who had learned a little about men, suggested the reason for their refusal was that they might be afraid of the ATS. After all she pointed out, we had organised the party project, now within days we were trying to coerce them into something else and she thought refusing was the men's way of rebelling against the threat of domination by females. She may have been right; we were surprised at their refusal especially from the Welshmen, but we asked permission which was granted.

We practised and practised, even tried a descant or two, but decided after some unfavourable comments by the non-singers to stick to plain singing and familiar carols. Setting out along the wet roads on Christmas morning, not marching but progressing tidily two by two in an easterly direction, a couple of police cars pulled up and asked us where we were going. When we told them they drove us right to the hospital doors. The four policemen opened the car doors with a flourish and saluted as they wished us a Merry Christmas, we felt like VIPs. Full of goodwill, if a little hoarse, we came out of the hospital later to meet the cold sleeting wind, but with the prospect of the festive meal awaiting us we stepped out smartly.

We experienced all the rigours of a hard winter on that site: snow, sleet, rain, wind, frost and fog. We didn't like the huts at all, barrack rooms they were really, housing the whole section. No stove in the centre to sit round and we felt deprived. The central heating which was turned on in the evening made hardly any difference, we still wore our greatcoats or teddy-bear outfits inside. Although we had been in uniform nearly three years, the weeks spent at Bailleston were the most dismal ever we all agreed. It never seemed to be daylight and our surroundings were cheerless. Life would have been more tolerable had the Army Education Service granted the courses.

Inspired by the results of the Happidrome venture, I made one or two more soft toys. Grey and white rabbits (not from socks) with enormous ears which prevented them from sitting up, made presents for the new offspring of friends at home. A sailor doll from fabric, which I intended to keep myself in memory of happy times in South Queensferry and Port Edgar Naval Base, Urquhart (Creighton) fell in love with, so I gave it to her; after all she had married one of the sailors.

Glasgow was too inconvenient for evening leave so we saved our pay for the 24-hr passes and mostly went to Edinburgh, though some enjoyable times were spent in Glasgow. It had a Locarno Ballroom, where a number of famous bands performed, cinemas and cafes. Sometimes concoctions offered on the menu were mysterious. Once Urquhart and I selected an interesting something, served in a tall glass similar to those used for Knickerbocker Glories. We were in the cafe part of the Locarno Ballroom in search of food at the time. Spooning the first mouthful with blissful anticipation, we looked across the table at each other. "Are you thinking what I'm thinking?" said Urquhart.

"Rice pudding, ice-cold rice pudding!" I exclaimed, "Well what a let down, I can't eat that," pushing the dish away disgustedly.

"Waste not want not," said Urquhart, "and besides we have paid for it, since when have you been able to chuck money away? It's not too bad, try it." I shuddered, perhaps if it had been my mother's rice pudding I might have eaten it, but ugh! I made do with a cup of tea.

Urquhart's mother and her sisters still at school had moved away from the bombing to Largs on the west coast. Her father, who worked in the city, looked after himself in the family house and spent weekends whenever he could down at Largs.

Urquhart also went to Largs on 24 hours which was nice for her, and how we envied her.

The rice pudding affair happened because the dance orchestra playing at the Locarno Ballroom was well known and it was a one-night performance which Urquhart didn't want to miss. She and I slept in the family house, her father was away in Largs, which was lucky for us she said for he would never have allowed us to be out so late. We scoffed a bag of Glasgow chips between us, walking along in the blackout after staying for the last waltz.

Girls and women were safe in city streets once, even in war time, strange as it may seem. Even with all the foreign soldiers and airmen about, the number of attacks on women were few. Fights naturally broke out, sometimes between nationalities, regiments and the three services, but they only happened in pubs and the Military Police were usually in the vicinity.

Urquhart was once coming back from a 24-hr leave and went to the toilets on the station before going to catch the bus to Baillieston when she was stopped by ATS Military Police. A London train was due to go out and there was always a lot of police activity about then. They asked her what she was doing on the station and whether she was going on the London train. If you were unlucky enough to be stopped by the Red Caps it always meant a cross examination. Wearing greatcoat and delving for her AB 64 which carried her identification among other things, to her horror she remembered leaving it on the dressing table at home. She told them this with a face that matched their hats, but the Red Caps told her to unbutton her greatcoat and look properly. She told us afterwards that she had considered making a run for it, but sensibly resisted the mad impulse.

When she unbuttoned her greatcoat she was wearing her kilt with her army tunic! Needless to say they whipped out their notebooks and took down all her particulars adding that she would be on a serious charge when their report was sent in. They waited while she turned out pocket, respirator, haversack and bag in the fruitless search for the AB 64. That meant another charge, no wonder she wasn't smiling after her 24 hours' leave.

Of course the rest of us laughed, although she had our sympathy we couldn't understand how she could possibly have forgotten her important identity papers. The kilt – well, with normal luck she wouldn't have been found out, for she planned only to wear it at dances, not under the auspices of the army. For days and days she went around with a worried look. When it seemed the dreaded summons to Battery Office would never come we all, after much speculation, decided that if anything was going to happen it would have happened. Because women in authority wearing uniform were still unaccepted by the majority of males, the report most probably ended up in the Battery Office waste paper basket.

Always, among our lot, events important or unimportant were discoursed upon, opinions stated and conclusions arrived at. Sometimes heated arguments ensued, but the majority decision was accepted even if privately some disagreed. When an issue had been settled and a policy adopted if the subject merited such measures, that was that – ours was a democratic group.

The bitter winter continued and on 15th January 1945, Jean Mann, a politician, held a lecture during the evening in the NAAFI. It was not compulsory to attend the lecture, but because she was a woman and not because any of us knew anything about real politics except Hague, we all turned up. The Coalition Government which ruled through most of the war years was coming to an end and elections took place while we were still at Baillieston. Labour won the election so would be the first government to face the difficult task of running the country when peace was ours again. All the votes for the services were postal so it took some time for the results to be made public.

Some time after the election, rumours again were heard about us moving. Raids were lessening somewhat, though we got a fair number of alarms during the night. "To keep us on our toes" was our conclusion when we'd given the matter our usual scrutiny after several false alarms.

Cliff Hanging

The rumour as always turned out to be truth; we moved again in darkness, ending up on the northeast coast of England at a tiny place with a church, a farm, a few cottages and a Boys' Brigade Summer camp – in peacetime that was – in wartime it was a gunsite. The now familiar Tracker Tower was installed beside the guns all on the edge of the cliffs. That part of the coast was being slowly eroded by wind and sea, due to the cliffs being sandy soil and the changing of the tides over the recent years. What had been a village was now under the waves like so many others on that coastline from Hornsea down to Spurn Point. The Command Post and guns seemed pretty near the edge. We hoped the ones who had sited them hadn't been too optimistic about the fury of the wind and the ocean. They sounded mighty threatening to us. We wished that we were still ignorant about the fate of the lost village.

The camp was basic, not expected to house people in winter and minus hot water. The ATS amenities, such as they were, consisted of a corrugated tin roof on poles with more corrugated tin fastened to the poles, which reached from ankle level. The rest was open to the elements, no door, only a doorway. Under the tin roof were six cold-water taps with basins. The toilets were one better than the ones on the marshes. A long wooden bench-type structure with holes similar to dry toilets but with a channel running below. At intervals there was a gushing of water along the channel – to where we knew not, from where we didn't enquire. One of our brainier members suggested that they may be a relic from

Roman times and how about writing to the newspaper about them. We told her we didn't think the newspaper would be interested. Hull had enough relics of its own, courtesy of the Luftwaffe. The toilets were separated by sacking but open at the front, all under the same tin roof and on the edge of the cliffs.

A privately run canteen instead of a NAAFI, which certainly did not have the same atmosphere as a NAAFI and was bedecked with notices which began "It is not allowed…". Not much was allowed, we discovered, our hearts sinking. When huts are dismal places, devoid of comfort, we look forward to a friendly welcoming NAAFI. To say the least we were not happy with our new home, it seemed to us that things were getting worse.

The huts, though the same size as the ones at Merrilees and Dalmeny, held twice as many beds, two-tiered rickety ones, even worse than the ones at Arborfield. The biscuits were so thin that you could feel the mesh wire through them. One solution was to lay the teddy-bear outfits underneath the biscuits, which made things a little better. There wasn't room for the ones in the bottom bunks to sit up in bed. The saying "packed like sardines" must have originated from those huts.

We had to rely on the official laundry collection. Baths too were restricted though Bath Parades started after a while. Fewer of us at a time were taken to the Public Baths in Hull, fortunately for us, still standing amidst the bomb damage.

While at Glasgow we had followed the manning procedure used before "Doodlebug Alley". At Mappleton the hours were changed again and the manning teams stayed at their posts for 48 hours. We were allowed to wear a blanket during the night; spotting was still a duty for all. On moonlit nights we had raids. One night when it was almost as light as day, the alarm sounded and D Section were manning. Some from our hut made the long trek to the tin shelter as we called it. That night was particularly frightening, the bombers accompanied by fighters roared overhead fairly low. The fighter planes zoomed down on the site, their guns spitting fire. On the bright concrete path we ran on towards the tin shelter and the bullets spattered on the tin roof as we dived inside under the sinks. Somehow we always felt safer when on manning duty, we were in just as much danger of course, but it always felt better because you were concentrating on the job in hand and you were hitting back, not just listening and waiting.

One day a message came through that some German prisoners had escaped. Prison camps in agricultural areas used the prisoners to work on farms. The ATS sentries were relieved by male guards armed with rifles. The men took over Guard duty for about a week until we learned that the prisoners had given themselves up. During that week it wasn't exactly pleasant at night up on the Command Post when strange footsteps would never have been heard above the roaring east wind.

PT took place on the cliffs just short of the barbed wire with the sea crashing below. None of us enjoyed it, what if our pounding feet, running on the spot to warm up, moved the sandy earth to collapse into the seething waves, muttered the grumblers. That included all of us, and as we went into breakfast, ravenous, I don't think it was imagination that made the meals seem smaller. We had never really suffered hunger on any site before, always ready for meals, not always relishing the menu, but never did anyone complain of not being full until Mappleton.

When Spring struggled through snow and ice the CO arranged, somehow from somewhere, the delivery of twelve bicycles (not new) for anyone on the site to use when on a pass. I don't remember whose brilliant idea it was from our hut (naturally it was from our hut, always in front where self-preservation was concerned), but a plan was put into operation forthwith.

Those who could ride cycles would, when on 24 hours' leave or evening pass, search through the lanes looking for farms and smallholdings. If the inevitable dog at the gate was protecting his master's property, the ATS were to hang about till someone came to investigate the barking. Then exude all the charm they could muster, be it man or woman who appeared and ask if they could buy a few eggs, pleadingly adding that cracked ones would do. If the dog was snarling with drooling jaws, the ATS were to withdraw with all haste.

As these tactics were being formulated, though all were in favour of the "egg run", surprisingly few seemed keen to face the unknown hazards. For a start, not everyone could ride a bicycle; one girl valiantly did learn to ride on the quiet lanes, but her purpose was mainly to get to somewhere without walking, buses were few and far between. There was the danger of geese, someone said, big birds with powerful wings that could break an arm or a leg.

"It's swans who can break bones, geese just run at you hissing with their necks stretched out to peck you," said another girl who was sitting on a top bunk cleaning her buttons.

"Shut up!" came from Odgers. "Do you want eggs or not?"

The one wielding the Brasso answered "No, I can do without eggs and anyway I can't ride a bike." She was not of the original dozen from Avalon because the whole of C Section were squashed into one hut and though we enjoyed a fairly peaceful and amicable relationship with the others, they were not as committed as we were to any joint plan or tactic.

If the forage was successful each person in the hut would be required to save a portion of her margarine ration and bread from the dining hall. The margarine was to cook the eggs, the bread was eaten dry. At least we had discovered a use for our mess tins. It didn't matter who faced the dogs, geese or any other danger as long as the cost of the eggs was shared and all the hut members took their turn in providing bread and fat. A roster was drawn up for the egg ration and meticulously adhered to. It was decided to execute the "egg run" in pairs and Odgers (who else with her charm) and I set off on the first of many forages. We returned intact without wounds from dogs or geese, carrying carefully six eggs (two of them cracked but still whole), and that evening six girl gunners cooked their own egg on the top of the stove in the centre of the hut. We had been glad to find the familiar black stove on our arrival at Mappleton, even if the rest of the furnishings were not desirable.

We didn't know how many rules we broke as the "egg run" continued, but in Army Rules and Regulations nothing was printed about ATS buying eggs, so we quietened our consciences, ignoring the fact that all food in civilian life was rationed. Needless to say complete secrecy about the venture was maintained.

A problem had to be faced: the fuel ration would cease in April so firewood still had to be accumulated. The risk of a fire being discovered was minimal for it didn't take many dry sticks to fry eggs. We didn't always manage to get six eggs but the supply was fairly regular and was a welcome supplement to our army ration. The canteen, unless anyone was really desperate, was not patronised by us.

The girl who had learned to ride a cycle could also ride a different steed. At home she rode horses, and finding out that they could be hired in Hornsea, she lost no time in sending for her riding clothes. Hornsea was our nearest town, a seaside town, a small friendly town. It had a handsome church, a few cosy little cafes, a Riding School, the Floral Hall, which was situated on the promenade and Hornsea Mere, the water of which was reputed to be one of the Ice-age lakes.

Apart from the visits to the public bath house, Hull did not see much of our battery, we preferred Hornsea. Through the efforts of our Lieutenant Emerson, we did enjoy visits to the theatre in Hull sometimes when a truck was organised to take us there and back. I remember seeing *Desert Rats* at the New Theatre in Hull. It was a fair distance to the bomb-ravaged city, buses ran only once a week; the service to Hornsea was sparse, hence the Battery bikes.

When the equestrian received her parcel, including boots and hard hat, she looked for someone to accompany her to the stables. One of the GL girls also had her riding things on site but the two of them were never on a 24-hr pass at the same time and she wouldn't go by herself. I thought Odgers might have been interested with her country-girl milkmaid looks but no, she said she was quite satisfied with the saddle of her bicycle, which in the meantime had been delivered from her home. Ever one to accept a challenge I told the would-be horsewoman that I'd accompany her to the stables, but if they didn't have a friendly horse then I would just watch. Pleased at last that she had a companion, she begged the loan of riding boots and hat for me. The boots fitted but not the hat.

I read or heard a quotation somewhere about women which

is very true: "Strange indeed are the ways of women". Gunner Brownlie seemed afraid to approach a riding stable on her own, Urquhart would not go down to the tin shelter alone in case she saw a rat (there were rats). If she wanted to use the toilet at night she'd wake Hague to accompany her. Others were afraid of dogs, geese, angry farmers and German parachutists and I was terrified of moths and spiders, yet none of us showed any fear whatsoever while a raid was in progress when on duty on the Command Post. Guns could be thundering beside us, the enemy threatening in the skies above us, but so totally immersed in our individual tasks were we, that the only emotion felt by us was desire to destroy that which we had been trained to destroy as quickly as possible. Soldiers down to the last shiny button, yet we never lost our femininity of our frailties.

Collecting cycles one dinner time and giving tunic buttons a last rub amid advice from all quarters about my forthcoming introduction to a four-legged friend, I listened to Brownlie. "Your hardest task will be to say in the saddle," said the expert. "Holding the reins and placing your feet correctly can be easily learned if you can only stay put." The others treated lightly the fact that I might be going into danger without a hard hat. They suggested I wear my steel helmet, which I suppose might not have been such a daft idea. Battledress would have to do, even though I ran the risk of being in trouble if I was seen wearing it out of camp. The ATS Military Police were only seen in large towns and cities so I wasn't too concerned about being found out. Unless I was thrown and received injuries resulting in medical attention pointed out someone, then if my trousers had to be cut away from the broken leg I wouldn't be able to conceal the fact that I was improperly dressed.

Our lives had become so dull that any little new happening had to be made the most of. Nothing funny had happened for ages so laughter was encouraged by fertile imaginations of what might happen in certain situations. We had not been granted the courses, no concert party had visited us since before "the marshes" and we hadn't felt like arranging our own. Although there was a concert hall beside the camp gate, no dances were held. It was only used for ABCA lectures and more discussions about what life may be like after demobilisation: enthusiasm seemed low on all sides. I, however, was light of heart as I joined in the jocularity about horses, Bob had asked me to marry him on his first leave and I had said yes. The date was unknown, for leave from overseas had not been granted. Only the army in Britain had resumed leave.

The girl who was to accompany us was waiting with horses already saddled, we quickly changed and went into the yard. I lost no time in telling the riding instructor that the only horses I knew were cart horses, so she said I'd better walk my mount, which she called a pony, round the yard a few times for us to get acquainted. I thought she meant me to walk holding the reins, but she meant me to sit on the pony while he walked and she would instruct me. The signal go left or right seemed simple enough, a pull on the right and the animal turned obediently and when I pulled on the left, he turned left. The trot needed a little more concentration. I was rising when I should have been descending, consequently it was uncomfortable till at last I got it right – well most of the time.

The instructor thought it was time we all left the ranch, there were only the three of us, as well as the horses of course. We were heading for the fields she told us, but were to follow her out of the gate for a little way along the main road. That worried me, or rather the traffic did. The pony behaved well of course, he was used to it. Little did I know that he was just biding his time until he felt the grass under his feet.

The instructor dismounted to open the gate into the field and motioned us to go through. While she was closing the gate my pony took off at a gallop with me clinging to mane and reins. I didn't know how to use the reins at that speed so I opted for what seemed the surest way to stay on. As I hung grimly on to his mane, hoping that he would soon tire, Brownlie galloped past looking confident. She was a tall girl and was on a horse with longer legs than my steed. They were both way in front when the instructor rode up alongside me shouting. I couldn't decipher her words for the noise of the pounding hooves. She galloped on to catch up with the other rider and I realised that we were supposed to be trotting, which is what we had been practising in the stable yard, but how was I to make the pony understand? Then in front I saw a figure flying through the air to land in long grass beside a hedge, her horse had stopped but the rider hadn't. I decided that I wouldn't try to make mine do anything, but would just let him carry on till he got fed up, trusting him not to jump anything. I was staying put but did not guarantee to stay put if he reared up over a hedge. When we reached the others my pony slowed down and stopped, enabling me to sit up and adjust the reins while waiting for a telling-off from the instructor for doing something wrong though I knew not what.

The instructor was busy making sure there were no broken bones, luckily the rider was unhurt. Her horse was quietly cropping grass as if he had nothing to do with the tumble. The instructor told us that the horses had not been ridden for some time, but she hadn't expected them to be as fresh. When all had remounted we set off at a walking pace towards the sea till we reached the barbed wire barriers. Shouts and whistles from a male RA Battery revealed to Brownlie and I that our guns were not the only ones in the area. We turned the horses and trotted all the way back to the main road without further mishap. I had thoroughly enjoyed my first experience and was to enjoy other pleasant rides with Brownlie and the riding instructor who was the daughter of the owner of the stables.

Stand Down

It was early in April when I had received Bob's proposal by letter; we hadn't seen each other since February '44. The Allied armies were only sixty miles away from Berlin and hard fighting was taking place. Many more men would be killed before it ended, everyone hoped with fervour that the end of the war was in sight.

My new home would be in Yorkshire near Wakefield; Bob would go back to work with his father in the family haulage business when he was demobbed. That much only was established, except that his mother was not pleased – she thought we were rushing things. My own mother kept her doubts to herself: she must have had them for she hadn't even met Bob, there had been no opportunity.

By then wartime weddings were commonplace. Families rallied, clothing coupons and points for rations were shared and a cake of some kind contrived. A borrowed white wedding dress was hanging covered in tissue paper, presents had begun to arrive at my home and Miss Neil, the ATS officer, had arranged for my leave to coincide with Bob's. When home leave for the forces in Europe was commenced, a date was arranged. My sister was to be bridesmaid in another borrowed dress.

A few days before my "big day" I received a letter from Bob saying it was all off. No explanation, just that he had changed his mind and goodbye. It was no consolation to me that it had happened to other girls, as my companions pointed out. I was devastated. They were not being cruel, just trying to help me come to terms with what had happened. The ATS officer said I could change the date of my leave if I wished, but I couldn't face the sympathy from the others so I wrote a brief note to my mother hoping it would arrive before I did and took my leave as arranged. I collected my leave pass and as I was packing in the hut no one said "have a good leave", the usual words, in fact no one said anything at all.

When I reached home (it had never seemed more welcoming to me as I almost ran down the lane), no one mentioned wedding, they all pretended that it was a normal leave. Mum told me afterwards that my face had a frozen look and none of them dared ask me any questions; she knew that I would talk to her eventually. I still hadn't shed a tear and didn't plan to, I only wished I knew why, why had he changed his mind?

The next day I returned wedding presents. Mum offered to do that as well as the ones that would have to be posted, but I said that I had to face everyone sometime and the sooner the better. It was no good running away from the fact that I had been jilted – jilted, it's a horrible word.

Living in a village meant that everyone knew all the happenings, good and bad, so it was no use skulking indoors afraid to meet people; besides I didn't want pity. Without the need of words I knew that my family were feeling for me. I wore uniform for the whole of that leave, it helped me somehow to get through the day and a stranger meeting me for the first time would never have guessed that my world had collapsed and that inside I had a deep hurt.

Still on leave, not really taking in any of the exciting news broadcasts from wireless bulletins or newspapers, wrapped in my own personal sorrow, I was unaware of the great events unfolding. When Winston Churchill announced on the 8th May 1945 that the long war was over and that Germany had surrendered, I felt no elation. The country went wild, flags flew and parties were held everywhere, jubilation unbounded. Forgotten by a few for a brief time was the war in the Far East where men were still dying. Two of my cousins were out there involved in jungle warfare and it was a long four months before the Japanese surrendered in September and the world knew peace.

The last day of my leave I cycled to one of my favourite spots.

Leaving the cycle in the hedge I walked through the woods and there among the trees I cried.

I returned to Mappleton the next day to find nothing changed except that the guns were silent. There was still marching drill, lectures on future methods of war, heaven forbid, discussions on life after demobilisation, Guard duty, fatigues, Fire Piquet and PT. I, however, had changed. Everyone in the hut refrained from asking questions. When I stopped using my evening pass they tried to coax me to go out. On a 24-hr pass I would go to the riding stables in the afternoon, but return to the site at teatime and in the morning would do the "egg run". I couldn't bear to be out in the evenings to see others enjoying life so stayed in reading.

One evening after tea when as usual I had made no plans to use my evening pass, a corporal from D Section knocked on the door of our hut and gave the normal shout "Can I come in?" before she entered and asked me to help her. She explained that three of them had dates with sailors, that evening transport was provided and they were to meet at a club in Hull. The corporal had just received a phone call asking if she could bring another girl as four sailors would be turning up. She said she had checked the evening leave list, saw my name and begged me to make a fourth to partner the other sailor. There would be dancing she added and it wouldn't cost me a penny. I refused, saying that I didn't go on blind dates, and was immediately assailed by cries from all present. In no uncertain terms they said I couldn't go on nursing a broken heart for ever, to stop throwing kindness in people's faces and that there had been a cloud hanging over our hut since I had returned form leave. They didn't know what to do about it or how to help me if I didn't want to be helped. Soft words and sympathy hadn't done any good and now it seemed they'd had enough. I felt ashamed, which is probably what they intended. In silence I got out my Brasso and brush. Telling me the time to be ready, the corporal left the hut. As I put on my cap, face devoid of make-up someone shouted, "Lipstick!" and threw one on to my bed. I used it and handed it back, another passed me a bottle of perfume, a true sacrifice in those days of shortages. As I went out of the door I felt, rather than heard, the sigh of relief behind me.

The evening was a dismal failure though I tried hard. Because we were in a crowd, my lack of sparkle was not so apparent as it might have been. The other girls, enjoying themselves, did not notice my disinterest and assumed that everyone was having a good time. The poor sailor who partnered me was under no such illusion, especially when he proved to have no skill as a dancer. Like a good many he thought it was only necessary to hold a girl close and walk to the music, and I must have shown that I wasn't impressed. I was thankful that we hadn't a late pass as we climbed into the truck and was glad the evening was over. I felt guilty about the poor sailor afterwards, but that night I was so miserable I didn't care. Arriving back to the bunch of blue-striped, flannelette clad, caring hut-mates, I answered in the affirmative to their questions about whether I'd enjoyed the evening. Without going into details I grabbed my sponge bag and went quickly down to the tin shelter where I waited till Lights Out before returning to the darkened and silent hut.

After that I made an effort to perk up. Slowly, I picked up the pieces and joined in arguments and discussions once more. To my surprise one day, a week after the outing to Hull, the same corporal from D Section told me to go to the gate as the sailor wanted to see me. I couldn't for the life of me see why and made some excuse. The corporal said he wanted to ask me out for that evening; his ship was leaving the next day. I found out later that the same group were going to the club again and they thought if my partner asked me personally to join them that I would accept. I simply refused to see him at that time, I wanted no involvement.

I did go with Stevenson and others of my own section to the Floral Hall at Hornsea which was on the promenade. Steps sled down from the hall to a strip of sand within the barbed-wire barricade. Hornsea had a nice wide sandy beach, which of course was out of bounds like all east coast beaches. A regular partner of mine at the dances was a soldier stationed in Hornsea and though I would never agree to meet him to go to the cinema or for a drink, I did look forward to meeting him at the Floral Hall: he was a marvellous dancer. I don't know how but he seemed to receive more than his fair share of soap coupons because he sometimes gave me a few.

One beautiful moonlight night at the end of an enjoyable tango (I am sure the band were playing *The White Dove*, it was a popular tune), he suggested that we took a walk along the strip of sand and down the steps we went. I knew my escort was a good bit older than I, but I was a little taken aback when he made it apparent that he expected certain favours from me on that moonlit beach in the shelter of a derelict boat. I soon put him straight on that score, thinking there goes my good dance partner, not to mention the soap coupons! There had been no romantic lead-up to this matter of fact proposal, so I admit to being surprised by it. "OK," he said, "we'll go back to the dance" and we did. The band was playing a lively quickstep and he whirled me onto the dance floor. I was still sure that I had lost a good partner and that he wouldn't ask me to dance again after that night. I didn't tell Stevenson about it then, thinking I'd save the incident until later when we could laugh about it with Urquhart.

It was then I discovered to my surprise, that I was sill capable of being amused and was looking forward to sharing laughter. The deep hurt was still there and would stay with me for ever, but from then on I was less of a wet blanket in the hut. The soldier continued to dance with me and kept on supplying me with soap coupons. After our battery had moved for the last time he wrote to me for ages, humorous letters about Hornsea and the offices he worked in. His letters always contained soap coupons.

It was in July that we packed for the last move. Arriving at Blackroad Camp on the outskirts of Leeds, we were surprised and not at all pleased to find German prisoners of war painting the huts. The accommodation was once more in great big barrack rooms housing a whole section. Although we were not packed like sardines, we would have preferred to remain in the packed huts at Mappleton while the fate of the battery was being decided.

All the four sections were housed at Blackroad Camp. Essential duties were carried out much the same. There were no manning parades of course and it was a relief to be on guard duty to escape from the cleaning fatigues, which seemed never ending. No fraternising with the prisoners was allowed – as if we wanted to fraternise, we said indignantly. Without guns and without any training taking place we couldn't see the need for the prisoners being there at all; anyway, there were enough of us to do all the painting as well as cleaning and grass cutting.

Mixed batteries were no longer required, so we were to be disbanded. The blow had fallen. After living together in all sorts of conditions as a closely knit unit for three and a half years, it was over. No farewell speeches, no end-of-term party. The army had its traditions but no room for sentiment; in any case the war in the Far East was not over. We were still in the army and would serve wherever we were ordered, but the girls felt as if they were being thrown on the scrap heap. The day we had to hand in Ack Ack kit to stores was like being stripped of our battle honours. No choice of jobs, the talk of re-training had been just empty talk. An inglorious end for 536 (m) Heavy Ack Ack Battery Royal Artillery, so thought the girl gunners.

Each day, lists of names were posted up with the date of the posting and where, but no detail of duties so no one knew their fate until they reached the end of their journey. The morning after your name appeared on the list you reported to Battery Office with your depleted kit, were handed a rail warrant and without ceremony climbed into an army utility truck to be dropped outside Leeds railway station. Day by day this went on, girls scattering to the north, south, east and west of Britain, filling gaps in various army depots until the split was absolute, and like the ten little nigger boys "then there were none" . . . .

All of this I recalled that spring day, standing on Romney Marsh.

Postscript

When the European war ended, married ATS girls were released, leaving gaps which were filled by discarded Ack Ack girls for the rest of the war and beyond. We were divided, but still united, then and now. Many 536 girls kept in touch after demob. and many of us managed to meet through the years.

I was attached to the Pay Corps in Ilfracombe, did a course there and worked in the Post Office Savings Bank, Army branch. We dealt with POWs' pay, savings accounts etc., updating them for their return to Britain.

Demobbed in the summer of 1946, to be home was so good because everyone was coming home. The crowds of young single people went about together: maybe it was because we had developed a herd instinct, having never been alone all that time we were in uniform. Eventually, couples began to pair off, but those first few months were a wonderful, carefree interlude that one can't explain to others – a coming-out-of-school, light-hearted feeling combined with the sheer joy of being alive. This, for me, is a special page in my memory book.

During this time I attended the christening of the Creighton baby, and was chief bridesmaid to an ATS cousin. In May 1947 I received a letter from Bob, asking me to meet him. We were married that year on September 13th and later blessed with a daughter and a son. Sadly, Bob died suddenly of a heart attack in 1980. I now have six grandchildren.

536 kept contact and in 1989 enjoyed, or e[illegible] together – those who could. We put back th[illegible]

were, the quiet ones still quiet, the noisy ones still noisy. This biennial reunion continued, but by 1993 it had developed into a full-scale reunion of batteries who revel in a joyful weekend. From Canada, America, Australia and New Zealand they come, to spend time with comrades of so long ago.

Vee Robinson
1996